Great Battles of World War Two

Battle of Stalingrad

Compiled by

Pandora Ruff

Scribbles

Year of Publication 2018

ISBN : 9789352979363

Book Published by

Scribbles

(An Imprint of Alpha Editions)

email - alphaedis@gmail.com

Produced by: PediaPress GmbH
Limburg an der Lahn
Germany
http://pediapress.com/

Contents

Prelude

Case Blue

Case Blue — German summer offensive of 1942	
Part of the Eastern Front of World War II	

German troops take cover behind a knocked out T-70 light tank and beside a Sd.Kfz. 250 halftrack, summer 1942

Date	28 June – 24 November 1942
Location	Voronezh, Rostov to Stalingrad, Kuban, Caucasus, Southern Russia, Soviet Union
Result	Axis operational failure

Belligerents

• Germany • Italy • Romania • Hungary • Croatia • Slovakia[1]	Soviet Union

Commanders and leaders

• Adolf Hitler[a] • Fedor von Bock • Maximilian von Weichs • Wilhelm List • Erich von Manstein • Paul von Kleist • Alexander Löhr • W. von Richthofen • Italo Gariboldi • Petre Dumitrescu • Ferenc Szombathelyi	• Joseph Stalin • Aleksandr Vasilevsky • Georgy Zhukov • Dmitri Kozlov • Ivan Tyulenev • Semyon M. Budenny • Filipp Golikov • Rodion Malinovsky • Andrey Yeryomenko • K. Rokossovsky • Semyon Timoshenko

Strength	

• **Initially:** 1,370,287 personnel
  • ▨ 1,210,861 men^2
  • ▪ 159,426 men^2
• 1,934 tanks and assault guns[b][3,2]
• 1,593–2,035 aircraft^2
	• **Totally:** 2,715,000 personnel
	  • Initially: 1,715,000 men^4
	  • 1,000,000 reserve
	• 2,959–3,720 tanks^4
	• c. 1,671 aircraft^5
	• 16,500 guns and mortars^4

Casualties and losses	
• 200,000 men^6 • 700 tanks destroyed^6	• 1,200,000 men^6 • 4,862 tanks destroyed^6

Case Blue (German: *Fall Blau*), later named **Operation Braunschweig**,[7] was the German Armed Forces' (*Wehrmacht*) name for its plan for the 1942 strategic summer offensive in southern Russia between 28 June and 24 November 1942, during World War II.

The operation was a continuation of the previous year's Operation Barbarossa, intended to knock the Soviet Union out of the war. It involved a two-pronged attack: one from the Axis right flank against the oil fields of Baku, known as Operation Edelweiss and one from the left flank in the direction of Stalingrad along the Volga River, known as Operation Fischreiher.[8]

Army Group South (*Heeresgruppe Süd*) of the German Army was divided into Army Groups A and B (*Heeresgruppe A* and *B*). Army Group A was tasked with crossing the Caucasus mountains to reach the Baku oil fields, while Army Group B protected its flanks along the Volga. Supported by 2,035 Luftwaffe aircraft and 1,934 tanks and assault guns, the 1,370,287-man Army Group South attacked on 28 June, advancing 48 kilometers on the first day and easily brushing aside the 1,715,000 Red Army troops opposite, who falsely expected a German offensive on Moscow even after *Blau* commenced. The Soviet collapse in the south allowed the Germans to capture the western part of Voronezh on 6 July and reach and cross the Don river near Stalingrad on 26 July. Army Group B's approach toward Stalingrad slowed in late July and early August owing to constant counterattacks by newly deployed Red Army reserves and overstretched German supply lines. The Germans defeated the Soviets in the Battle of Kalach and the combat shifted to the city itself in late August. Nonstop Luftwaffe airstrikes, artillery fire and street-to-street combat completely destroyed the city and inflicted heavy casualties on the opposing forces. After three months of battle, the Germans controlled 90% of Stalingrad on 19 November.

In the south, Army Group A captured Rostov on 23 July and swept south from the Don to the Caucasus, capturing the demolished oilfields at Maikop on 9 August and Elista on 13 August near the Caspian Sea coast. Heavy Soviet resistance and the long distances from Axis sources of supply reduced the

Axis offensive to local advances only and prevented the Germans from completing their strategic objective of capturing the main Caucasus oilfield at Baku. Luftwaffe bombers destroyed the oilfields at Grozny but attacks on Baku were prevented by the insufficient range of the German fighters.

The possibility that the Germans would continue to the south and east, and possibly link up with Japanese forces (then advancing in Burma) in India, was of great concern to the Allies. However, the Red Army defeated the Germans at Stalingrad, following Operations Uranus and Little Saturn. This defeat forced the Axis to retreat from the Caucasus. Only the Kuban region remained tentatively occupied by Axis troops.

Axis strategy

Background

On 22 June 1941 the Wehrmacht had launched Operation Barbarossa with the intention of defeating the Soviets in a Blitzkrieg lasting only months. The Axis offensive had met with initial success and the Red Army had suffered some major defeats before halting the Axis units just short of Moscow (November/December 1941). Although the Germans had captured vast areas of land and important industrial centers, the Soviet Union remained in the war. In the winter of 1941–42 the Soviets struck back in a series of successful counteroffensives, pushing back the German threat to Moscow. Despite these setbacks, Hitler wanted an offensive solution, for which he required the oil resources of the Caucasus.[9] By February 1942 the German Army High Command (OKH) had begun to develop plans for a follow-up campaign to the aborted Barbarossa offensive – with the Caucasus as its principal objective. On 5 April 1942, Hitler laid out the elements of the plan now known as "Case Blue" (*Fall Blau*) in *Führer* Directive No. 41. The directive stated the main goals of the 1942 summer campaign on Germany's Eastern Front: holding attacks for Army Group (AG) Centre, the capture of Leningrad and the link-up with Finland for AG North, and the capture of the Caucasus region for Army Group South. The main focus was to be the capture of the Caucasus region.[10,11]

The oilfields

The Caucasus, a large, culturally diverse region traversed by its eponymous mountains, is bounded by the Black Sea to the west and the Caspian Sea to the east. The region north of the mountains was a production center for grain, cotton and heavy farm machinery, while its two main oilfields, at Maykop, near the Black Sea, and Grozny, about halfway between the Black and the Caspian Seas, produced about 10 percent of all Soviet oil. South of the mountains lay Transcaucasia, comprising Georgia, Azerbaijan and Armenia. This heavily industrialized and densely populated area contained some of the largest oilfields in the world. Baku, the capital of Azerbaijan, was one of the richest, producing 80 percent of the Soviet Union's oil—about 24 million tons in 1942 alone.[12]

The Caucasus also possessed plentiful coal and peat, as well as nonferrous and rare metals. Manganese deposits at Chiaturi, in Transcaucasia, formed the richest single source in the world, yielding 1.5 million tons of manganese ore annually, half of the Soviet Union's total production. The Kuban region of the Caucasus also produced large amounts of wheat, corn, sunflower seeds, and sugar beets, all essential in the production of food.

These resources were of immense importance to Hitler and the German war effort. Of the three million tons of oil Germany consumed per year, 85 percent was imported, mainly from the United States, Venezuela, and Iran. When war broke out in September 1939, the British naval blockade cut Germany off from the Americas and the Middle East, leaving the country reliant on oil-rich European countries such as Romania to supply the resource. An indication of German reliance on Romania is evident from its oil consumption; in 1938, just one-third of the 7,500,000 tons consumed by Germany came from domestic stocks. Oil had always been Germany's Achilles heel, and by the end of 1941, Hitler had nearly exhausted Germany's reserves, which left him with only two significant sources of oil, the country's own synthetic production and the Romanian oilfields, with the latter supplying 75% of Germany's oil imports in 1941.[13] Aware of his declining oil resources, and fearful of enemy air attacks on Romania (Germany's main source of crude oil), Hitler's strategy was increasingly driven by the need to protect Romania and acquire new resources, essential if he wanted to continue waging a prolonged war against a growing list of enemies. In late 1941, the Romanians warned Hitler that their stocks were exhausted and they were unable to meet German demands. For these reasons, the Soviet oilfields were extremely important to Germany's industry and armed forces as the war became global, the power of the Allies grew, and shortages started to occur in Axis resources.[14,15]

Planning

Axis forces

The offensive was to be conducted across the southern Russian (Kuban) steppe utilizing the following Army Group units:[16]

- Army Group A, under Wilhelm List (Caucasus campaign)
  - First Panzer Army
  - Seventeenth Army

Bundesarchiv, Bild 101III-Altstadt-056-12
Foto: Altstadt | 1942 Sommer

Figure 1: *Waffen-SS infantry and armour advancing, Summer 1942*

- Third Romanian Army[e]
- Eleventh Army[f]
- Army Group B, under Maximilian von Weichs (Volga campaign)
  - Second Army
  - Fourth Panzer Army
  - Sixth Army
  - Second Hungarian Army
  - Fourth Romanian Army
  - Eighth Italian Army
- *Luftflotte 4*, under Alexander Löhr
  - 8th Air Corps
  - 4th Air Corps

German air strength in the east numbered 2,644 aircraft on 20 June 1942, over 20% more than a month earlier. Whereas in 1941 most units fought on the central front supporting Army Group Centre, 1,610 aircraft (61%), supported Army Group South. Initially commanded by Löhr, on 20 July 1942, Wolfram Freiherr von Richthofen took command of *Luftflotte 4*.[17]

The German plan involved a three-staged attack:[18,19]

- *Blau I*: Fourth Panzer Army, commanded by Hermann Hoth (transferred from Army Group North) and the Second Army, supported by the Second Hungarian Army, would attack from Kursk to Voronezh and continue the advance, anchoring the northern flank of the offensive towards the Volga.

- *Blau II*: Sixth Army, commanded by Friedrich Paulus, would attack from Kharkov and move in parallel with Fourth Panzer Army, to reach the Volga at Stalingrad (whose capture was not deemed necessary).
- *Blau III*: First Panzer Army would then strike south towards the lower Don River, with Seventeenth Army on the western flank and Fourth Romanian Army on the eastern flank.

The strategic objectives of the operation were the oilfields at Maykop, Grozny and Baku. As in Barbarossa, these movements were expected to result in a series of grand encirclements of Soviet troops.[20]

Soviet forces

The Soviet army command (*Stavka*) failed to discern the direction of the main German strategic offensive anticipated in 1942, even though they were in possession of the German plans. On 19 June, the chief of operations of the 23rd Panzer Division, Major Joachim Reichel, was shot down over Soviet-held territory while flying an observation aircraft over the front near Kharkov. The Soviets recovered maps from his aircraft detailing the exact German plans for Case Blue. The plans were handed over to *Stavka*, in Moscow.[21]

Joseph Stalin, however, believed it to be a German ruse,[22] remaining convinced that the primary German strategic goal in 1942 would be Moscow, in part due to Operation Kremlin (*Fall Kreml*), a German deception plan aimed at the city. As a result, the majority of Red Army troops were deployed there, although the direction from which the Case Blue offensive would come was still defended by the Bryansk, Southwestern, Southern and North Caucasian Fronts. With about 1 million soldiers at the front line and another 1.7 million in reserve armies, their forces accounted for about one quarter of all Soviet troops.[23,24] Following the disastrous start of Case Blue for the Soviets, they reorganised their frontlines several times. Over the course of the campaign, the Soviets also fielded the Voronezh Front, Don Front, Stalingrad Front, Transcaucasian Front, and the Caucasian Front, though not all existed at the same time.

With the German thrust expected in the north, *Stavka* planned several local offensives in the south to weaken the Germans. The most important of these was aimed at the city of Kharkov and would be conducted mainly by the Southwestern Front under Semyon Timoshenko, supported by the Southern Front commanded by Rodion Malinovsky. The operation was scheduled for 12 May, just prior to a planned German offensive in the area.[25] The ensuing Second Battle of Kharkov ended in disaster for the Soviets, severely weakening their mobile forces.[26] At the same time, the Axis clearing of the Kerch Peninsula

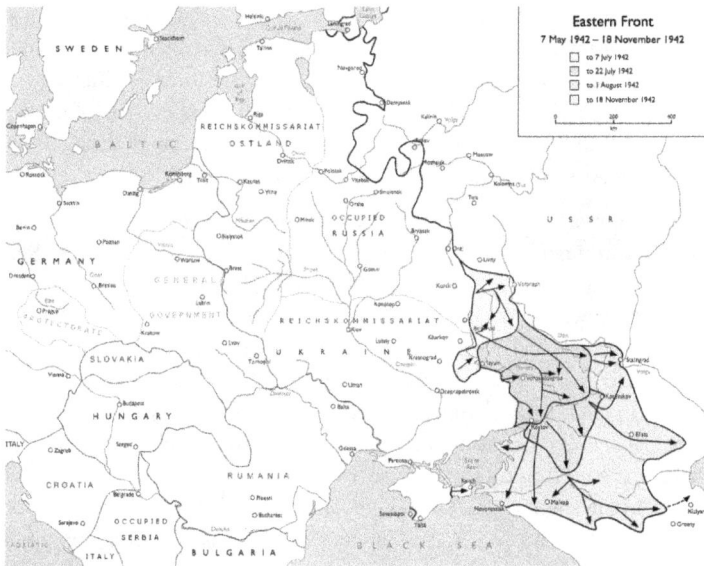

Figure 2:
The German advance from 7 May to 18 November 1942.
to 7 July
to 22 July
to 1 August
to 18 November

together with the Battle of Sevastopol, which lasted until July, weakened the Soviets further and allowed the Germans to supply Army Group A across the Kerch Peninsula through the Kuban.[27]

The offensive

Opening phase

The German offensive commenced on 28 June 1942, with Fourth Panzer Army starting its drive towards Voronezh. Due to a chaotic Soviet retreat, the Germans were able to advance rapidly, restoring *Wehrmacht* confidence for the upcoming major offensive.[28]

Close air support from the Luftwaffe also played an important role in this early success. It contained the Red Air Force, through air superiority operations, and provided interdiction through attacks on airfields and Soviet defence lines. At times, the German air arm acted as a spearhead rather than a support force, ranging on ahead of the tanks and infantry to disrupt and destroy defensive positions. As many as 100 German aircraft were concentrated on a single Soviet division in the path of the spearhead during this phase. General Kazakov, the Bryansk Front's chief of staff, noted the strength and effectiveness of the Axis aviation.[29] Within 26 days, the Soviets lost 783 aircraft from the 2nd, 4th, 5th and 8th Air Armies, compared to a German total of 175.[30]

By 5 July, forward elements of Fourth Panzer Army had reached the Don River near Voronezh and became embroiled in the battle to capture the city. Stalin and the Soviet command still expected the main German thrust in the north against Moscow, and believed the Germans would turn north after Voronezh to threaten the capital. As a result, the Soviets rushed reinforcements into the town to hold it at all costs and counterattacked the Germans' northern flank in an effort to cut off the German spearheads. 5th Tank Army, commanded by Major General A.I. Liziukov, managed to achieve some minor successes when it began its attack on 6 July, but was forced back to its starting positions by 15 July, losing about half of its tanks in the process.[31] Although the battle was a success, Hitler and von Bock, commander of Army Group South, argued over the next steps in the operation. The heated debate, and continuing Soviet counterattacks, which tied down Fourth Panzer Army until 13 July, caused Hitler to lose his temper and dismiss von Bock. As part of the second phase of the operation, on 9 July, Army Group South was split into Army Group A and Army Group B, with Wilhelm List appointed as commander of Army Group A in place of von Bock.

Only two weeks into the operation, on 11 July, the Germans began to suffer logistical difficulties, which slowed the advance. The German Sixth Army was continually delayed by fuel shortages. Eight days later, on 20 July, shortages of fuel were still undermining operations, leaving many units unable to execute their orders. The 23rd Panzer Division and 24th Panzer Division both became stranded during the opening phase. Once again, as it had done during the Norwegian Campaign in April 1940, and *Barbarossa* in 1941, the Luftwaffe's Junkers Ju 52 transport fleet flew in supplies to keep the army going. The situation remained difficult with German troops forced to recover fuel from damaged or abandoned vehicles, and in some cases, leave behind tanks and vehicles with heavy fuel consumption to continue their advance. This undermined the strength of the units, which were forced to leave fighting vehicles behind. Nevertheless, the Luftwaffe flew in 200 tons of fuel per day to keep the army supplied.[32] Despite this impressive performance in keeping the army mobile, Löhr was replaced by the more impetuous and offensive-minded von Richthofen.[33]

Splitting of Army Group South

Believing that the main Soviet threat had been eliminated, desperately short of oil and needing to meet all the ambitious objectives of Case Blue, Hitler made a series of changes to the plan in *Führer* Directive No. 45 on July 23, 1942:

* reorganized Army Group South into two smaller Army Groups, A and B;
* directed Army Group A to advance to the Caucasus and capture the oil fields (Operation Edelweiß);
* directed Army Group B to attack towards the Volga and Stalingrad (Operation Fischreiher).[8]

There is no evidence Hitler was opposed by, or received complaints from Franz Halder, Chief of the General Staff, or anyone else, about the directive until August 1942. The new directive created enormous logistical difficulties, with Hitler expecting both Army Groups to advance along different routes. Logistics lines were already at breaking point with ammunition and fuel shortages most apparent and it would be impossible to advance using the conservative supply rates he demanded. The divergence of the Army Groups would also open a dangerous gap between the Armies, which could be exploited by the Soviets. The Italian Alpine Corps, of the Italian Army in the Soviet Union, did not arrive in the Caucasus Mountains with Army Group A, instead remaining with Sixth Army. Army Group A was expected to operate in mountain terrain with only three mountain divisions and two infantry divisions unsuited to the task.[34]

The splitting of Army Group South enabled the launching of Operation Edelweiss and Operation Fischreiher, the two main thrusts of the Army Groups. Both groups had to achieve their objectives simultaneously, instead of consecutively.[8] The success of the initial advance was such that Hitler ordered the Fourth Panzer Army south to assist the First Panzer Army to cross the lower Don river.[35] This assistance was not needed and Kleist later complained that Fourth Panzer Army clogged the roads and that if they had carried on toward Stalingrad, they could have taken it in July. When it turned north again two weeks later, the Soviets had gathered enough forces together at Stalingrad to check its advance.[36]

Figure 3: *German troops and a Sd.Kfz. 251 armored half-track on the Russian steppe, August 1942*

Army Group A: Caucasus

Breaking into the Caucasus

With air support from the Ju 87s of *Sturzkampfgeschwader 77*, List's Army Group A recaptured Rostov, the "gate to the Caucasus", on 23 July 1942 relatively easily.[37] The *Luftwaffe* had air superiority in the early phase of the operation, which was of great help to the ground forces.[38] With the Don crossing secured and Sixth Army's advance flagging on the Volga front, Hitler transferred the Fourth Panzer Army to Army Group B and sent it back to the Volga.[39] The redeployment used enormous amounts of fuel to transfer the army by air and road.[40]

After crossing the Don on 25 July, Army Group A fanned out on a 200 km (120 mi) front from the Sea of Azov to Zymlianskaya.[41] The German Seventeenth Army, along with elements of the Eleventh Army and the Romanian Third Army, manoeuvred west towards the east coast of the Black Sea, while the First Panzer Army attacked to the south-east. The Seventeenth Army made a slow advance but the First Panzer Army had freedom of action. On 29 July the Germans cut the last direct railway between central Russia and the Caucasus, causing considerable panic to Stalin and Stavka, which led to the passing of Order No. 227 "Not a step back!".[42] Salsk was captured on 31 July and Stavropol on 5 August. Although the army group made a quick advance, by 3

August the vanguard comprised only light mobile forces and most of the tanks lagged behind, due to lack of fuel and supply breakdowns, despite the efforts of 4th Air Corps, which flew in supplies around the clock.

On 9 August, the First Panzer Army reached Maikop in the foothills of the Caucasus mountains, having advanced more than 480 kilometres (300 mi) in fewer than two weeks. The western oil fields near Maikop were seized in a commando operation from 8–9 August, but the oil fields had been sufficiently destroyed by the Red Army to take about a year to be repaired. Shortly afterwards Pyatigorsk was taken. On 12 August, Krasnodar was captured and German mountain troops hoisted the Nazi flag on the highest mountain of the Caucasus, Mount Elbrus.[43]

The length of the German advance created chronic supply difficulties, particularly of petrol; the Black Sea was judged too dangerous and fuel was brought by rail through Rostov or delivered by air, but panzer divisions were sometimes at a standstill for weeks. Even petrol trucks ran out of fuel and oil had to be brought up on camels.[44] With the Soviets often retreating instead of fighting, the number of prisoners fell short of expectations and only 83,000 were taken.[45] As Hitler and OKH began to concentrate on Stalingrad, some of Kleist's mobile forces were diverted. Kleist lost his flak corps and most of the *Luftwaffe* supporting the southern front, only reconnaissance aircraft being left behind. The Voyenno-Vozdushnye Sily (VVS) brought in about 800 bombers, a third of which were operational. With the transfer of air cover and flak units, Soviet bombers were free to harass the German advance.[46] The quality of the Soviet resistance increased, with many of the forces used coming from local levies, who Kleist thought were willing to fight harder for their homeland.[46] German units were especially bogged down by fighting Georgian alpine and mountain troops, who greatly contributed to stalling their advance. The quantity of replacements and supplies the Soviets committed increased, and faced with these difficulties, the Axis advance slowed after 28 August.[47,48]

Battle for the oilfields

In the south-east, the *Wehrmacht* headed in the direction of Grozny and Baku, the other important petroleum centres. More installations and industrial centres fell into German hands, many intact or only slightly damaged during the Russian retreat. From August–September, the Taman Peninsula and a part of the Novorossiysk naval base were captured.[49] The Germans continued towards Tuapse on the Black Sea coast and in the east Elista was taken on 13 August.[50] In the south, the German advance was stopped north of Grozny, after taking Mozdok on 25 August.[51] German paratroopers assisted an insurgency in Chechnya, operating behind Soviet lines. German mountain troops failed to

Figure 4: *German Gebirgsjäger in the Caucasus*

secure the Black Sea ports and the advance fell short of Grozny as supply difficulties arose once more. The Soviets dug in the 9th and 44th armies of the
North Transcaucasian Front along the rocky Terek River bank in front (north)
of the city. The *Luftwaffe* was unable to support the German army that far
forward and Soviet aviation attacked bridges and supply routes virtually un-
opposed. The Germans crossed the river on 2 September but made only slow
progress.[52] At the beginning of September, Hitler had a major argument with
the High Command and specifically List, as he perceived the advance of the
German forces as too slow. As a result, Hitler dismissed List on 9 September
and took direct command of Army Group A himself.[53]

Axis ships transported 30,605 men, 13,254 horses and 6,265 motor vehicles
across the Black Sea from Romania, from 1–2 September. With the reinforcements, the Germans captured most of the Black Sea naval bases but were
held up at Novorossiysk, where the Soviet 47th Army had prepared for a long
siege.[54] The port fell on 10 September, after a four-day battle, the final German victory in the Caucasus. It left the heights south of the port and several coast roads in the hands of 47th Soviet Army. Attempts to push out of
Novorossiysk were costly failures and the Axis also failed to break the defences
on the coastal plain from Novorossiysk to Tuapse, having only the strength to
stabilise the line. Romanian Army losses were particularly high and the Romanian 3rd Mountain Division was nearly wiped out by a Soviet counter-attack
from 25–26 September.[55]

Figure 5: *German Gebirgsjäger operating a 2 cm anti-aircraft gun in the Central Caucasus near Teberda, September 1942*

Further east, the Axis enjoyed greater success and on 1 September, the Germans took Khulkhuta (Хулхутá), halfway between Elista and Astrakhan.[56] During August and September, German patrols raided the railway between Kizlyar, north-east of Grozny, marking the farthest advance of the German forces towards the Caspian Sea.[57] In the south, the First Panzer Army advance on Grozny was stopped by the Red Army and the 14th Air Army. By late September, supply failures and the resistance of the Red Army slowed the Axis advance.[58]

On 2 November 1942, Romanian mountain troops (*Vânători de munte*) under the command of Brigadier General Ioan Dumitrache took Nalchik, the capital of Kabardino-Balkaria and also the farthest point of Axis advance into the Caucasus. This victory earned the Romanian General the Knight's Cross of the Iron Cross.[59] Up to 10,000 prisoners were captured in two days, before the advance toward Grozny was stopped again west of the city at Vladikavkaz.[60] On 5 November, Alagir was seized and the Alagir–Beslan–Malgobek line reached became the farthest German advance in the south.[61] By this time, the gap between Army Groups A and B had left them vulnerable to a counter-offensive. Only the German 16th Motorized Infantry Division remained inside the gap, guarding the left flank of the First Panzer Army by securing the road towards Astrakhan.[62] On 22 November, after several Soviet counter-attacks, Hitler appointed Kleist as Group commander with orders to hold his position and prepare to resume the offensive if Stalingrad could be taken.

Luftwaffe oil offensive

In the first week of October 1942, Hitler came to recognise that the capture of the Caucasus oil fields was unlikely before winter forced the Germans to take up winter positions. Unable to capture them, he was determined to deny them to the enemy and ordered the *Oberkommando der Luftwaffe* (OKL) to inflict as much damage as possible.[63]

On 8 October, Hitler called for the air offensive to be carried out no later than 14 October, as he required air assets for a major effort at Stalingrad.[64] As a result, on 10 October 1942, *Fliegerkorps* 4 of *Luftflotte* 4 (4th Air Corps of Fourth Air Fleet) was ordered to send every available bomber against the oilfields at Grozny. Fourth Air Fleet was in poor shape by this time – von Richthofen had begun Case Blue with 323 serviceable bombers out of a total of 480. He was now down to 232, of which only 129 were combat ready. Nevertheless, the force could still deliver damaging blows. Attacks on the refineries reminded von Richthofen of the attacks on Sevastopol several months earlier. Thick black smoke rose from the refineries to a height of 5,500 metres (18,000 ft). On 12 October, further raids caused even more destruction. It had been a strategic mistake not to have made greater efforts to hit the oil refineries at Grozny and Baku sooner, as their destruction would have been a greater blow to the Soviets than the loss of Stalingrad, where most of the air fleet was deployed. On 19 November, the Soviet counter-offensive at Stalingrad compelled von Richthofen to once more withdraw his units north to the Volga and bring an end to the aerial offensive.[65]

Much damage was done at Grozny, but the remaining oilfields were beyond the logistical reach of the German Army as well as the fighter aircraft of the Luftwaffe. Grozny was within range of German bombers from 4th Air Corps, based near the Terek River. But Grozny and the captured oilfields at Maykop produced only ten per cent of Soviet oil. The main fields at Baku were out of German fighter range. German bombers could have reached them, but it meant flying the most direct, thus most predictable route without protection. In August it may have been possible to carry out these operations owing to the weakness of Soviet air power in the region, but by October it had been considerably strengthened.[66]

Figure 6: *Advance towards Stalingrad at the Don*

Army Group B: Volga

Don bend

On 23 July, the main body of Army Group B started its advance toward the Don. The Germans met with increasing Soviet resistance from the new Stalingrad Front, with the 62nd and 64th Soviet Armies. On 26 July, XIV Panzer Corps broke through and reached the Don, where the new First and Fourth Tank Armies conducted several futile counter-attacks by inexperienced troops. In the south, Fourth Panzer Army made better progress against 51st Army. After crossing the Don, the Germans advanced on Kotelnikovo, reaching the town by 2 August. Soviet resistance convinced Paulus that Sixth Army was not strong enough to cross the Don by itself, so he waited for Fourth Panzer Army to fight its way north.[67] On 4 August, the Germans were still 97 km (60 mi) from Stalingrad.[68]

By 10 August, the Red Army had been cleared from most of the west bank of the Don, but Soviet resistance continued in some areas, further delaying Army Group B. The *Wehrmacht* advance on Stalingrad was also impeded by supply shortages caused by the poor state of Soviet roads. The *Luftwaffe* sent an ad-hoc force of 300 Ju 52 transport aircraft, enabling the Germans to advance; some bombers were diverted from operations to supply flights under the *Stalingrad Transport Region force*. The Soviet defence at the Don forced the Germans to commit more and more troops to an increasingly vulnerable front, leaving few reserves to back up the Axis divisions on either flank.[69] The

Figure 7: *A Ju 87 Stuka dive bomber over Stalingrad*

Soviets made several counter-attacks on the northern flank of Army Group B, between Stalingrad and Voronezh. From 20–28 August, the 63rd Army and the 21st Army counter-attacked near Serafimovich, forcing the Italian Eighth Army to fall back. The 1st Guards Army attacked near Novo-Grigoryevskaja, extending its bridgehead. These and several other bridgeheads across the Don, opposed by the Eighth Italian and Second Hungarian armies, were a constant danger.

On 23 August, Sixth Army crossed the Don and Army Group B established a defensive line on one of its bends. Sixth Army reached the northern suburbs of Stalingrad later that day, beginning the Battle of Stalingrad. The Hungarian, Italian and Romanian armies were 60 km (37 mi) from Stalingrad, which was in range of forward air bases. *Luftflotte* 4 attacked the city, turning much of it to rubble.[70] The Soviets reported that civilian casualties from 23–26 August were 955 dead and 1,181 wounded (a preliminary total; later reports of casualties in the tens of thousands were probably exaggerations).[71]

Sixth Army advanced from the north via Kalach and Fourth Panzer Army came up from the south through Kotelnikovo. In the first few days, the XIV Panzer Corps opened a corridor between the main body of Sixth Army and the northern Stalingrad suburbs at the Volga. In the south, Soviet resistance repulsed the Fourth Panzer Army. On 29 August another attempt was made with Hoth

Figure 8: *Street fighting in the destroyed city*

turning his forces west directly through the center of 64th Army. The attack was unexpectedly successful and Fourth Panzer Army got behind 62nd and 64th Armies with the chance to encircle and cut off 62nd Army. Von Weichs ordered Sixth Army to complete the encirclement; a Soviet counter-attack held up the advance for three days and the Soviets escaped and retreated towards Stalingrad.[72] The rapid German advance caused a slump in morale among the Soviet troops, who retreated in chaos, abandoning the outer defences of the city.[73] After defeating the last Soviet counter-attacks, Sixth Army resumed its offensive on 2 September, linking up with Fourth Panzer Army the following day. On 12 September, the Germans entered Stalingrad.[74]

Battle of Stalingrad

The advance into Stalingrad against the 62nd Army was carried out by Sixth Army, while Fourth Panzer Army secured the southern flank. The city was a 24 km (15 mi) ribbon along the west bank of the Volga, which forced the Germans to conduct a frontal assault, and the ruins of the city gave the defenders an advantage. To counter *Luftwaffe* air superiority, the commander of the 62nd Army, General Vasily Chuikov, ordered his troops to "hug" the Germans, negating German tactical mobility. The *Luftwaffe* suppressed Soviet artillery on the east bank of the Volga and caused many casualties during Soviet attempts to reinforce the defenders on the west bank. From mid-September until early November the Germans made three big attacks on the city and ground forward in mutually-costly fighting. By mid-November, the

Soviets were penned into four shallow bridgeheads, with the front line only 180 m (200 yd) from the river. Anticipating victory, substantial numbers of *Luftwaffe* aircraft were withdrawn to the Mediterranean in early November to support the Axis operations in Tunisia. Sixth Army had captured about 90 percent of the city.[75],[76]

On 19 November, the Soviets launched Operation Uranus, a two-pronged counter-offensive against the flanks of Sixth Army. With the battle for the city and the exhaustion of Fourth Panzer Army, the flanks were mainly guarded by Romanian, Hungarian and Italian soldiers. Third Romanian Army, on the Don River west of Stalingrad, and Fourth Romanian Army, south-east of Stalingrad, had been under constant Soviet attack since September. Third Romanian Army had been transferred from Caucasus on 10 September to take over Italian positions on the Don, opposite the Soviet bridgeheads. The Romanians were understrength and had only around six modern anti-tank guns per division. The bulk of the German tank reserve, the 48th Panzer Corps, consisted of about 180 tanks, half being obsolete Panzer 35(t)s.[77] The two Romanian armies were routed and Sixth Army with parts of Fourth Panzer Army were encircled in Stalingrad.[78]

Hitler ordered Sixth Army to remain on the defensive, rather than try to break out. It was intended the army would be supplied by air, but the quantity of supplies necessary was far beyond the ability of the *Luftwaffe* to carry. Sixth Army's strength diminished and the Soviets gained the upper hand inside the city.[79] To stabilise the situation on the Eastern Front, Army Group Don (*Heeresgruppe Don*) under Field Marshal Erich von Manstein was created to fill the gap between Army Groups A and B.[80] On 12 December, a relief operation called Operation Winter Storm was launched from the South by fresh reinforcements of the 4th Panzer Army. The offensive surprised the Soviets and the Germans were able to penetrate the Soviet line for 50 km (31 mi) towards Stalingrad. Despite these gains, the Sixth Army was not allowed to attempt to break out and link up, so this led to nothing.[81] The failure was followed by a siege that lasted for almost three months, during which Sixth Army was destroyed.[82]

Figure 9: *Soviet forces during Operation Little Saturn*

Aftermath

Operation Saturn

Following the success of Operation Uranus, the Red Army began Operation Saturn to cut off Army Group A and all troops east of Rostov.[83] During the German relief operation at Stalingrad, Soviet forces had been redeployed, lesser objectives substituted, and the operation renamed "Little Saturn". The attack fell on Eighth Italian Army and the remnants of Third Romanian Army, and led to the destruction of most of Eighth Army. On the verge of collapse, Army Groups B and Don were able to prevent a Soviet breakthrough but Army Group A was ordered to withdraw from the Caucasus on 28 December.[84,85]

The Soviets launched several follow-up offensives, later called the Voronezh-Kharkov Strategic Offensive. The Ostrogozhsk–Rossosh Offensive began on 12 January and destroyed large parts of the Second Hungarian Army and the remnants of Eighth Italian Army at the Don south-east of Voronezh. With the southern flank in danger, Second German Army was forced to withdraw from Voronezh and the Don. The operations continued until January and led Stavka to believe that they could deal a fatal blow to the Germans and decide the war in southern Russia. Operation Star, conducted by the Voronezh Front, was aimed at Kharkov, Kursk and Belgorod. Operation Gallop was conducted by the South-western Front against Voroshilovgrad, Donetsk and then towards the Sea of Azov, to cut off the German forces east of Donetsk. The operations began simultaneously at the end of January. The Soviets broke through quickly and in the north, Kursk fell on 8 February and Kharkov on 16 February after a German withdrawal, while in the south the Germans were pushed back to a line west of Voroshilovgrad. Army Groups Don, B and parts of Army Group A [g] were renamed Army Group South, commanded by Manstein, on 12 February.

The Kharkov and Donbas operations were started on 25 February by the new Central Front led by Rokossovsky, with the forces freed after the surrender of the Germans in Stalingrad on 2 February. The operations were aimed at Army Group Centre in the north and timed to coincide with the expected successes of the Soviet operations in the south. Army Group South escaped encirclement and prepared a counter-offensive, which led to the Third Battle of Kharkov and the stabilisation of the front.[86,87] The disaster at Stalingrad was the end of Case Blue and the territorial gains had been reversed by the end of 1943, except for the Kuban bridgehead on the Taman peninsula, retained for a possible second offensive to the Caucasus, which was held until 9 October 1943.[88,89]

Analysis

Due to the initial success of the German summer offensive in 1942, Hitler and the German commanders became more ambitious, putting great strain on the German army. Hitler did not expect the Soviets to be able to launch a counter-offensive as big as Operation Uranus and sent troops elsewhere, ordering the *Wehrmacht* to simultaneously achieve several goals. Opposition led to Hitler sacking dissenters and interfering more in command.[90,91]

Overextension reduced the capabilities of the German Army and its allies to defend this territory and the Soviets mounted a decisive offensive at Stalingrad, encircling a German army. Soon both sides concentrated on the battle for the city, making Caucasus a secondary theatre. With Army Group B unable to hold the Volga line, Soviet offensives almost cut off Army Group A in Caucasus and it was forced to withdraw. The surrender of Sixth Army was a huge blow to German morale and it came as a great shock to Hitler. Despite the destruction of Sixth Army, the Soviets were only able to force the German Army back from Caucasus, delaying the final decision on the Eastern Front. The Soviet command overestimated its capabilities and pushed its forces forward to the limit of its supply lines, which led to defeat at the Third Battle of Kharkov and left the Germans able to fight the Battle of Kursk in the summer of 1943.[92]

Notes

- **a** Army Group A was under direct command of the *OKH* from 10 September 1942 until 22 November 1942, when von Kleist took over.
- **b** Not all of those tanks were serviceable at the beginning of the offensive, as tanks were in repair, already engaged in combat, refitting, or not present at the frontline.
- **c** The Third Romanian Army was later assigned to Army Group B and was one of the two Romanian armies heavily engaged in Operation Uranus.
- **d** After the successful completion of the battle for the Kerch Peninsula, 11th Army was split and only parts of it were assigned to Army Group A.
- **e** The Seventeenth Army of Army Group A stayed in the Kuban bridgehead.

Bibliography

- Antill, Peter (2007). *Stalingrad 1942*. Oxford: Osprey Publishing. ISBN 1-84603-028-5.
- Axworthy, Mark; Scafes, Cornel; Craciunoiu, Cristian (1995). *Third Axis Fourth Ally: Romanian Armed Forces in the European War, 1941–1945*. London: Arms & Armour Press. ISBN 1-85409-267-7.
- Beevor, Antony (1999). *Stalingrad: The Fateful Siege: 1942–1943*. London: Penguin Books. ISBN 0-14-028458-3.
- Bellamy, Chris (2007). *Absolute War: Soviet Russia in the Second World War*. London: Pan Books. ISBN 978-0-330-48808-2.
- Bergström, Christer (2007). *Stalingrad – The Air Battle: November 1942 – February 1943*. London: Chervron/Ian Allen. ISBN 978-1-85780-276-4.
- Glantz, David M.; Jonathan M. House (2009). *To the Gates of Stalingrad: Soviet-German Combat Operations, April–August 1942*. The Stalingrad Trilogy. **I**. Lawrence, KS: University Press of Kansas. ISBN 978-0-7006-1630-5.
- Glantz, David M. (1995). *When Titans Clashed: How the Red Army Stopped Hitler*. Lawrence, KS: University Press of Kansas. ISBN 0-7006-0899-0.
- Hayward, Joel (1995). *Too Little Too Late: An Analysis of Hitler's Failure in 1942 to Damage Soviet Oil Production*. Lawrence, KS: The Journal of Strategic Studies, Vol. 18, No. 4, pp. 94–135.
- Hayward, Joel (2001). *Stopped at Stalingrad: The Luftwaffe and Hitler's Defeat in the East, 1942–1943*. Lawrence, KS: University Press of Kansas. ISBN 0-7006-1146-0.

- Holt, David (June 2009). "The Slovak Army: 1939 – 1945 Part 2: The Russian Campaign 1940 – 43"[93] (PDF). *Journal of The Czechoslovak Philatelic Society of Great Britain*. **27** (2). ISSN 0142-3525[94]. Retrieved 18 February 2014.
- Javrishvili K., Battle of Caucasus: Case for Georgian Alpinists, Translated by Michael P. Willis, 2017.
- Liddell Hart, Basil Henry (1948). *The German Generals Talk*. New York: Morrow. ISBN 0688060129.
- Liedtke, Gregory (2016). *Enduring the Whirlwind: The German Army and the Russo-German War 1941-1943*. Helion and Company. ISBN 978-0-313-39592-5.
- Mercatante, Steven (2012). *Why Germany Nearly Won: A New History of the Second World War in Europe*. Praeger. ISBN 978-1910777756.
- Nipe, George M. Jr. (2000). *Last Victory in Russia: The SS-Panzerkorps and Manstein's Kharkov Counteroffensive—February–March 1943*. Atglen, PA: Schiffer Publishing. ISBN 0-7643-1186-7.
- Schramm, Percy Ernst (1963). *Kriegstagebuch des Oberkommandos der Wehrmacht, 1940–1945 Teilband II*. Bonn: Bernard & Graefe Verlag für Wehrwesen.
- Wegner, Bernd (1990). "Der Krieg gegen die Sowjetunion 1942/1943 [The war against the Soviet Union 1942/43]". In Boog, Horst; Rahn, Werner; Stumpf, Reinhard; Wegner, Bernd. *Der globale Krieg: Die Ausweitung zum Weltkrieg und der Wechsel zur Initiative 1941 bis 1943 [The Global War: The expansion of the war into a world war and the change of initiative]*. Germany and the Second World War (in German). **VI**. *Militärgeschichtliches Forschungsamt*. Deutsche Verlags-Anstalt. pp. 761–1094. ISBN 3-421-06233-1.

Orders of battle

Axis order of battle at the Battle of Stalingrad

The **Axis order of battle at Stalingrad** is a list of the significant land units that fought in the Battle of Stalingrad on the side of the Axis Powers between September 1942 and February 1943.

Apart from the twenty divisions of the German Wehrmacht, eighteen Romanian divisions and one Croatian regiment took part in the battle on the Axis side as well.

Order of battle

In December 1942, the German 6th Army, under the command of Generaloberst (promoted January 1943 to Generalfeldmarschall) Friedrich Paulus had the following Order of Battle:

German

- **Army Troops**
  - 648th Army Signal Regiment
  - 2nd Nebelwerfer Regiment
  - 30th Nebelwerfer Regiment
  - 51st Mortar Regiment
  - 53rd Mortar Regiment
  - 91st Air Defence Regiment
  - 243rd Assault Gun Battalion
  - 245th Assault Gun Battalion
  - 45th Army Engineer Battalion
  - 225th Army Engineer Battalion

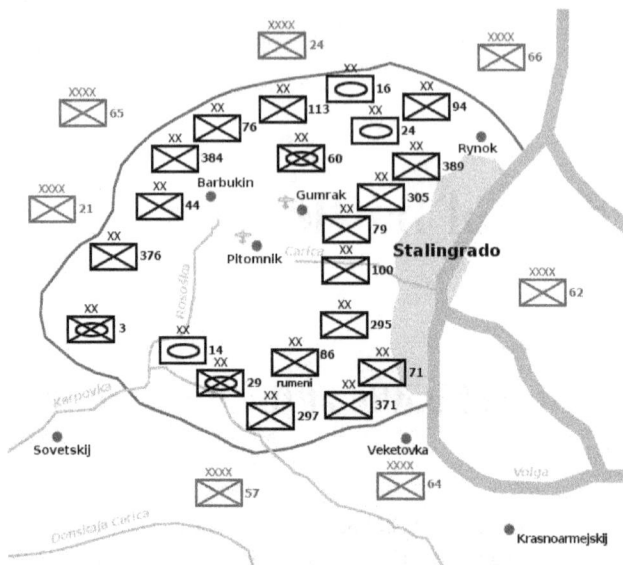

Figure 10: *Map of the Stalingrad pocket, following Operation Uranus, showing all Axis Divisions and major Soviet Divisions*

- 294th Army Engineer Battalion
- 336th Army Engineer Battalion
- 501st Army Engineer Battalion
- 605th Army Engineer Battalion
- 652nd Army Engineer Battalion
- 672nd Army Engineer Battalion
- 685th Army Engineer Battalion
- 912nd Army Engineer Battalion
- 921st Army Engineer Battalion
- 925th Army Engineer Battalion
- **IV Army Corps** - General der Pioniere Erwin Jaenecke, from 17 January General der Artillerie Max Pfeffer
  - 29th Motorized Infantry Division - Generalmajor Hans-Georg Leyser
  - 297th Infantry Division - General der Artillerie Max Pfeffer, from 16 January Generalmajor Moritz von Drebber
  - 371st Infantry Division - Generalleutnant Richard Stempel
- **VIII Army Corps** - General der Artillerie Walter Heitz
  - 76th Infantry Division - Generalleutnant Carl Rodenburg
  - 113th Infantry Division - Generalleutnant Hans-Heinrich Sixt von Armin

- **XI Army Corps** - General der Infanterie Karl Strecker
  - 44th Infantry Division - Generalleutnant Heinrich-Anton Deboi
  - 376th Infantry Division - Generalleutnant Alexander Edler von Daniels
  - 384th Infantry Division - Generalleutnant Eccard Freiherr von Gablenz, from 16 January Generalmajor Hans Dörr
- **XIV Panzer Corps** - General der Panzertruppe Hans-Valentin Hube, from 17 January Generalleutnant Helmuth Schlömer
  - 3rd Motorized Infantry Division - Generalmajor Helmuth Schlömer, from 18 January Oberst Jobst Freiherr von Hanstein
  - 60th Motorized Infantry Division - Generalmajor Hans-Adolf von Arenstorff
  - 16th Panzer Division - Generalleutnant Günther Angern
- **LI Army Corps** - General der Artillerie Walther von Seydlitz-Kurzbach
  - 71st Infantry Division - Generalleutnant Alexander von Hartmann, from 25 January Generalmajor Fritz Roske
  - 79th Infantry Division - Generalleutnant Richard Graf von Schwerin
  - 94th Infantry Division - Generalleutnant Georg Pfeiffer
  - 100th Jäger Division - Generalleutnant Werner Sanne
  - 295th Infantry Division - Generalmajor Otto Korfes
  - 305th Infantry Division - Generalleutnant Bernhard Steinmetz
  - 389th Infantry Division - Generalmajor Erich Magnus, from 19 January Generalmajor Martin Lattmann
  - 14th Panzer Division - Generalmajor Martin Lattmann
  - 24th Panzer Division - Generalleutnant Arno von Lenski
- **Luftwaffe**
  - 9th Flak-Division - Generalmajor Wolfgang Pickert
  - Jagdgeschwader 3 - Wolf-Dietrich Wilcke

Romanian

- **Third Army** - General Petre Dumitrescu
  - 1st Cavalry Division - General de Brigadă Constantin Brătescu;
  - 7th Cavalry Division
  - 5th, 6th, 7th, 9th, 11th, 13th, 14th and 15th Infantry Divisions
  - 1st Armoured Division
  - various Artillery Regiments
- **Fourth Army** - General de Corps Constantin Constantinescu-Claps
  - 1st, 2nd, 4th and 18th Infantry Divisions
  - 20th Infantry Division - General de Divizie Nicolae Tătăranu to January 1943, then General de Divizie Romulus Dimitriu;
  - 5th and 8th Cavalry Divisions

Croatian

- 369th Reinforced Infantry Regiment (attached to 100th division) - Colonel Viktor Pavičić, later Lieutenant-Colonel Marko Mesić.[95]

External links

- Lexikon der Wehrmacht[96] (in German)
- Commanders at the Battle of Stalingrad[97] (in Dutch)
- The 6th Army order of Battle[98]
- Map of Stalingrad - 12 December 1942[99]
- Stalingrad Order Of Battle[100]

Soviet order of battle for the Battle of Stalingrad

The **Soviet order of battle for the Battle of Stalingrad** details the major combat units that fought in the Battle of Stalingrad. This shows the Soviet order of battle on 19 November 1942, the beginning of Operation Uranus.

Red Army Order of Battle

STAVKA Representatives

- Army General G.K. Zhukov
- Colonel-General of Artillery N.N. Voronov
- Colonel-General A.M. Vasilevsky[101]:435

Stalingrad Front

The Stalingrad Front, under the command of Colonel General Andrey Yeryomenko, assisted by Political Officer Nikita Khrushchev, included the following units:[101]:435–437

- 8th Air Army (General Timofey Khryukin)
- 28th Army (Lieutenant General Dmitry Ryabyshev)
  - Rifle Divisions: 34th Guards, 248th
  - Special Brigades: 52nd, 152nd, 159th
  - Tank Brigades: 6th Guards
  - Front Reserve: 330th Rifle Division, 85th Tank Bde
- 51st Army (General N.I. Trufanov)
  - Rifle Divisions: 15th Guards, 91st, 126th, 302nd

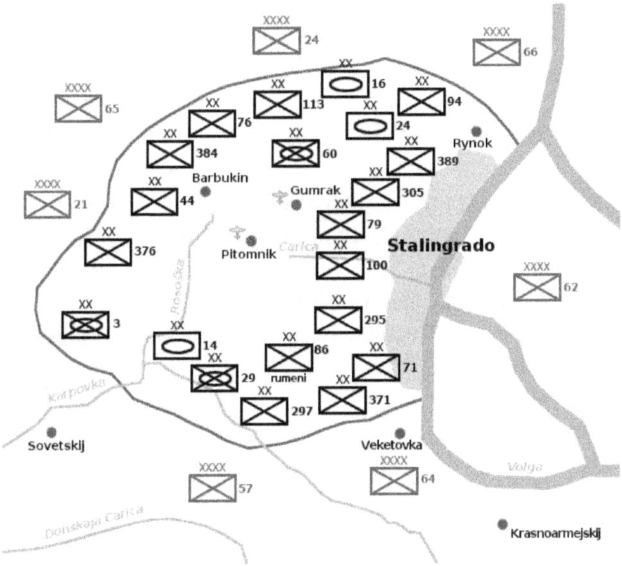

Figure 11: *Map of the Stalingrad pocket, following Operation Uranus, showing all Axis Divisions and some Soviet Divisions*

- Special Brigades: 38th
- Tank Brigades: 254th
- Armoured formations added for Operation Uranus: 4th Mechanised Corps, 4th Cavalry Corps
- 57th Army (General F.I. Tolbukhin)
  - Rifle Divisions: 169th, 422nd
  - Special Brigades: 143rd
  - Tank Brigades: 90th, 235th
  - Armoured formations added for Operation Uranus: 13th Mechanized Corps
- 62nd Army (General V.I. Chuikov)
  - Rifle Divisions: 13th Guards, 37th Guards, 39th Guards, 45th, 95th, 112th, 138th, 193rd, 196th, 244th, 284th, 308th, 10th NKVD
  - Naval Infantry Brigades: 92nd
  - Special Brigades: 42nd, 115th, 124th, 149th, 160th
  - Tank Brigades: 84th, 137th, 189th
- 64th Army (General M.S. Shumilov)
  - Rifle Divisions: 36th Guards, 29th, 38th, 157th, 204th
  - Naval Infantry Brigades: 154th
  - Special Brigades: 66th, 93rd, 96th, 97th

- Tank Brigades: 13th, 56th

Don Front

Colonel General Konstantin Rokossovsky's Don Front included the following
units:[101]:437

- 24th Army (General I.V. Galanin)
  - Rifle Divisions: 49th, 84th, 120th, 173rd, 233rd, 260th, 273rd
  - Tank Brigades: 10th
- 65th Army (General Lieutenant-General P.I. Batov)
  - Rifle Divisions: 4th Guards, 27th Guards, 40th Guards, 23rd, 24th,
    252nd, 258th, 304th, 321st
  - Tank Brigades: 121st
- 66th Army (Major-General A.S. Zhadov)
  - Rifle Divisions: 64th, 99th, 116th, 226th, 299th, 343rd
  - Tank Brigades: 58th
- 16th Air Army (Major-General S.I. Rudenko)

Southwestern Front

The Southwestern Front, commanded by Army General Nikolai Vatutin, included the following units:[101]:437–438

- 1st Guards Army (General D.D. Lelyushenko)
  - Rifle Divisions: 1st, 153rd, 197th, 203rd, 266th, 278th
  - Front Reserve: 1st Guards Mechanised Corps
- 5th Tank Army (General P.L. Romanenko)
  - Rifle Divisions: 14th Guards, 47th Guards, 50th Guards, 119th, 159th,
    346th
  - Armoured formations added for Operation Uranus: 1st Tank Corps,
    26th Tank Corps, 8th Cavalry Corps
- 21st Army (Major-General Ivan Chistyakov)
  - Rifle Divisions: 63rd, 76th, 96th, 277th, 293rd, 333rd
  - Tank Regiments: 4th Guards, 1st, 2nd
  - Armoured formations added for Operation Uranus: 4th Tank Corps,
    3rd Guards Cavalry Corps
- 2nd Air Army (Colonel K. Smirnov)[102]
- 17th Air Army (Major-General S.A. Krasovsky)

Bibliography

- Beevor, Antony (1998). *Stalingrad*. Viking, London. ISBN 978-0-14-103240-5.

Attack on Stalingrad

Bombing of Stalingrad

Stalingrad, a Soviet city and industrial centre on the river Volga, was bombed heavily by the Luftwaffe during the Battle of Stalingrad in World War II. German land forces comprising the 6th Army had advanced to the suburbs of Stalingrad by August 1942. The city was firebombed with 1,000 tons of high explosives and incendiaries in 1,600 sorties on 23 August. The destruction was monumental and complete, turning Stalingrad into a sea of fire and killing thousands of civilians and soldiers. Further fire-attacks were mounted against the ruined city for the next two days, enveloping it in dense volcano-like black smoke clouds that stretched 3.5 kilometers into the sky.

In accordance with Adolf Hitler's demand to exterminate all traces of Soviet resistance, Soviet forces hiding in the rubble were subjected to nonstop German airstrikes until the Soviet counteroffensive in late November 1942. *Luftflotte 4* flew 1,000 sorties per day on average from 23 August to 22 November, the bulk of which were directed at Stalingrad.

Background

Luftwaffe General Martin Fiebig's *Fliegerkorps VIII* was tasked in July 1942 with providing air support for the German 6th Army and 4th Panzer Army as they captured Stalingrad and secured the northern flank of the German advance to the Caucasus oilfields.[103]

Fiebig's superior's, *Generaloberst* Wolfram von Richthofen's *Luftflotte 4* held a 1,600 kilometer eastern frontage in July and concentrated its efforts on Stalingrad, with the air support missions in the Caucasus under Kurt Pflugbeil's *Fliegerkorps IV* and at the Voronezh battle being given a lower priority. Logistics for *Fliegerkorps VIII* received the highest preference, as Richthofen saw the capture of Stalingrad as the key to German success on the entire Eastern

Bundesarchiv, Bild 183-J17815
Foto: Klose | Oktober 1942

Figure 12: *The ruins of Stalingrad on 2 October 1942.*

Front. Richthofen requested additional Junkers Ju 52 transport groups from *Oberkommando der Luftwaffe* and transferred Pflugbeil's groups, as well as his road transport companies, to the administrative authority of a new, specially created, "Stalingrad transport region". He also ordered better procedures and greater efforts to maximize efficiency. His activities bore fruit as the Luftwaffe constantly lifted ammunition, provisions and fuel to the front. The army (*Heer*) implemented its own initiatives to increase supply effectiveness, the insufficient perfection of which had undermined the speed of the German advance since the beginning of Case Blue in June. By the third week of August, the 6th Army and *Fliegerkorps VIII* were receiving sufficient supplies to undertake without undue difficulties their primary mission of capturing Stalingrad.[104]

Prelude

During the Battle of Kalach, *Fliegerkorps VIII* provided the German XIV and XXIV Panzer Corps' with decisive air support as the Soviet 62nd Army was encircled and destroyed west of Kalach from 8–11 August through the application of superior German firepower from all sides and especially from above. 50,000 prisoners were taken by the Germans, 1,100 Soviet tanks were destroyed or captured and the road to Stalingrad was laid bare.[105]

LI Army Corps penetrated across the Don north of Kalach on 21 August, forcing the surprised and helpless Red Army formations to the south to fall back on

Stalingrad. XIV Panzer Corps crossed the Don the next morning across two enormous pontoon bridges created by German engineers. Fiebig's air corps shot down 139 Red aircraft in three days and inflicted massive damage on Soviet ground forces. On 21 August Richthofen personally flew across the Don in his Fieseler Fi 156 and was shocked at the carnage of dead Soviet bodies and destroyed tanks. Hours after Richthofen's sightseeing, *Kampfgeschwader 76*'s Junkers Ju 88 medium bombers exterminated two surprised Soviet reserve divisions on open fields 150 kilometers east of Stalingrad. Richthofen was excited and delighted by the one-sided massacre and wrote in his diary: "Blood flowed!"[106]

Within two days of crossing the Don, Gustav Anton von Wietersheim's XIV Panzer Corps rolled forth to reach the Volga river at Spartanovka in the northern suburbs of Stalingrad at 1600 hours on 23 August. Stavka, the Soviet supreme command, was shocked by the speed of Wietersheim's advance. It was accomplished largely thanks to an overwhelming deluge of German airpower. *Fliegerkorps VIII* flew 1,600 unbroken sorties, blasting a path for the Panzer spearheads by dropping 1,000 tons of bombs on 23 August. Junkers Ju 87 *Stuka* dive bombers, Focke-Wulf Fw 190 ground attack aircraft and Heinkel He 111 and Junkers Ju 88 medium bombers bombed and strafed the paralyzed Soviets, landed, refueled, restocked their ordnance and flew more missions as the German aircraft never broke the cycle. *Fliegerkorps VIII* lost only three aircraft that day (against Soviet claims of 90), while destroying 91 Soviet aircraft in a single day and inflicting immeasurable damage on the Soviet soldiers and civilians on the ground.[107]

The destruction of Stalingrad

It was only the first half of *Fliegerkorps VIII*'s attacks that day as the second great air offensive of 23 August was carried out against the city of Stalingrad itself. From 3:18 pm on 23 August 1942 and through the night into 24 August units of *Generaloberst* von Richthofen's *Luftflotte 4* constantly attacked the city. Medium Bomber strength employed included elements of KG 27, KG 51, KG 55, KG 76, and I/KG 100.[108]*

During 23 August *Luftflotte 4* flew approximately 1,600 sorties and dropped 1,000 tons of bombs on the city effectively destroying it, while three aircraft were lost. Buildings crumbled under the blast effects of high explosives, while the extensive use of incendiaries torched factories, schools and houses. Wooden houses were immediately incinerated, leaving only their chimneys on the surface. In the first few hours of bombing, the headquarters of the city's air defenses were bombed. Stalingrad was enveloped in dense, volcano-like black clouds of smoke that stretched 3,500 meters into the sky. The destruction was

Figure 13: *Soviet women with their belongings amidst the firebombed ruins of Stalingrad on 24 August.*

monumental and complete as the entire city was put on fire and Soviet families either died or fled to ravines north of the city to escape the holocaust descending on their homes. Giant flames rose to the sky from massive destroyed oil storage containers and fuel tankers, which also spilled their contents of burning oil into the Volga, where it danced on the surface. The city was quickly turned to rubble, although some factories survived and continued production whilst workers militia joined in the fighting.[109]

After 23 August, Stalingrad was bombed block-by-block for a further five days. According to official statistics the Soviet fighter defences of 8 VA and 102 IAD PVO claimed 90 German planes shot down, in addition to 30 by anti-aircraft defense. The Soviet Air Force in the immediate area lost 201 aircraft from 23–31 August, and despite meager reinforcements of some 100 aircraft in August, it had 192 servicable aircraft, which included 57 fighters. The burden of the initial defense of the city fell on the 1077th Anti-Aircraft (AA) Regiment.Wikipedia:Citation needed

After another day of heavy bombing on 24 August, Richthofen on the morning of 25 August flew personally over the city to watch the "great fire-attack" of the day. He later wrote that the city was completely destroyed without any worthwhile further targets. In the evening, Soviet searchlights illuminated the

Figure 14: *Children's Dance fountain in Stalingrad on 24 August 1942.*

sky as the city burned bright, spewing smoke and flames into the sky, a sight that *Generalmajor* Wolfgang Pickert, commander of the 9th Flak Division, described as "fantastic".[110]

Stalin resisted the evacuation of civilians, in part due to the importance of the city's factories to the war effort. Initial Soviet reports stated the water supply and electricity grid as knocked out. On 26 August a detailed Soviet *Urban Committee of Defence* report gave the following casualty figures; 955 dead and 1,181 wounded.[111] Due to the fighting that followed and the high death toll, it is impossible to know how many more were killed in aerial attacks. The figure was higher than in the initial reports but reports of 40,000 dead in the three-day raid are not credible. As air-raid shelters in the city were extremely inadequate for the population of the Soviet metropolis and large portions of the suburban buildings were made of easily-flammable wood, the death toll and destruction from the bombing was comparable to the British bombing of Darmstadt on 11/12 September 1944, when 900 tons of bombs from 226 Avro Lancaster heavy bombers killed 12,300 German citizens of the city.[109]

Further operations

Wietersheim's isolated Panzer Corps was subjected to heavy Soviet counterattacks, which threatened to destroy it. *Fliegerkorps VIII* once again rescued its *Heer* comrades, launching nonstop attacks on the Red Army and stopping its

Bundesarchiv , Bild 146-1978-093-03
Foto: Niermann I 1942

Figure 15: *An industrial plant in Stalingrad
on 16 November 1942, destroyed by Stukas.*

attacks in their tracks. Richthofen, who was disgusted by the army's lack of ag-
gressiveness, demanded an immediate, all-out attack to take the city. Hermann
Hoth's 4th Panzer Army, immobilized for days far to the south of Stalingrad
due to a lack of fuel, recommenced its offensive on 28 August with strong
support from the Stukas and Fw 190s of *Fliegerkorps VIII*. Hoth's Panzer Divisions outflanked the Soviets on 29 August, who fell back on Stalingrad. On
30 August Richthofen, believing the fall of Stalingrad to be imminent, ordered
fresh terror attacks on the city to break the Soviet will to resist. That day and
the next, *Fliegerkorps VIII* launched full-scale bombing operations against the
city, also attacking Soviet airfields east of the Volga to maintain German air
superiority.[112]

Luftflotte 4 defeated the VVS in the airspace above the city, restricting the
Soviets to night operations. The Germans obtained daylight air superiority
over the Stalingrad area and exploited their edge to devastating effect. From
5 to 12 September, *Luftflotte 4* conducted 7,507 sorties (938 per day). From
16 to 25 September, it carried out 9,746 sorties (975 per day). On 14 October
it launched 1,250 sorties against Soviet positions west and east of the Volga
and Soviet traffic along the river. That same day, its three Stuka *Geschwader*
mounted 320 sorties against the Soviet positions on the west bank, dropping
540 tons of bombs on them.[113]

Over the course of the battle through to late 1942, the Germans flew 70,000 sorties dropping over a million bombs.Wikipedia:Citation needed

References

Citations

Bibliography

- Hayward, J. (1998). *Stopped At Stalingrad: The Luftwaffe and Hitler's Defeat in the East, 1942–1943*. Lawrence, Kansas: University Press of Kansas. ISBN 978-0-7006-1146-1.

Operation Uranus: the Soviet offensive

Operation Uranus

Operation *Uranus*	
Part of the Battle of Stalingrad on the Eastern Front of World War II	
Date	19–23 November 1942
Location	Near Stalingrad (now Volgograd) 48°42′N 44°31′E[114]Coordinates: 48°42′N 44°31′E[114]
Result	Decisive Soviet victory Encirclement of Axis forces
Belligerents	
Soviet Union	Germany Italy Romania Hungary
Commanders and leaders	
Joseph Stalin Semyon Timoshenko Konstantin Rokossovsky Aleksandr Vasilevsky Nikolai Vatutin	Adolf Hitler Friedrich Paulus Petre Dumitrescu

Strength	
1,143,500 personnel (including reserve) 894 tanks 13,451 artillery pieces 1,500 aircraft	**German**: 250,000+ personnel unknown number of artillery pieces 732 aircraft (402 serviceable) **Italian**: 220,000 personnel unknown number of artillery pieces or aircraft **Romanian**: 143,296 personnel 827 artillery pieces 134 tanks unknown number of aircraft **Hungarian**: 200,000 personnel unknown number of artillery pieces or tanks
Casualties and losses	
Unknown	Unknown

Operation *Uranus* (Russian: Операция «Уран», romanised: Operatsiya "Uran") was the codename of the Soviet 19–23 November 1942 strategic operation in World War II which led to the encirclement of the German Sixth Army, the Third and Fourth Romanian armies, and portions of the German Fourth Panzer Army. The operation was executed at roughly the midpoint of the five month long Battle of Stalingrad, and was aimed at destroying German forces in and around Stalingrad. Planning for Operation *Uranus* had commenced in September 1942, and was developed simultaneously with plans to envelop and destroy German Army Group Center (Operation Mars) and German forces in the Caucasus. The Red Army took advantage of the German army's poor preparation for winter, and the fact that its forces in the southern Soviet Union were overstretched near Stalingrad, using weaker Romanian troops to guard their flanks; the offensives' starting points were established along the section of the front directly opposite Romanian forces. These Axis armies lacked heavy equipment to deal with Soviet armor.

Due to the length of the front created by the German summer offensive, aimed at taking the Caucasus oil fields and the city of Stalingrad, German and other Axis forces were forced to guard sectors beyond the length they were meant to occupy. The situation was exacerbated by the German decision to relocate several mechanized divisions from the Soviet Union to Western Europe. Furthermore, units in the area were depleted after months of fighting, especially those which took part in the fighting in Stalingrad. The Germans could only count on the XXXXVIII Panzer Corps, which had the strength of a single panzer division, and the 29th Panzergrenadier Division as reserves to bolster their Romanian allies on the German Sixth Army's flanks. In comparison, the Red Army deployed over one million personnel for the purpose of beginning the offensive in and around Stalingrad. Soviet troop movements were not without problems, due to the difficulties of concealing their build-up, and to Soviet units commonly arriving late due to logistical issues. Operation *Uranus* was first postponed from 8 to 17 November, then to 19 November.

At 07:20 Moscow time on 19 November, Soviet forces on the northern flank of the Axis forces at Stalingrad began their offensive; forces in the south began on 20 November. Although Romanian units were able to repel the first attacks, by the end of 20 November the Third and Fourth Romanian armies were in headlong retreat, as the Red Army bypassed several German infantry divisions. German mobile reserves were not strong enough to parry the Soviet mechanized spearheads, while the Sixth Army did not react quickly enough nor decisively enough to disengage German armored forces in Stalingrad and reorient them to defeat the impending threat. By late 22 November Soviet forces linked up at the town of Kalach, encircling some 290,000 men east of the Don River. Instead of attempting to break out of the encirclement, German leader Adolf Hitler decided to keep Axis forces in Stalingrad and resupply them by air. In the meantime, Soviet and German commanders began to plan their next movements.

Background

On 28 June 1942, the Wehrmacht began its offensive against Soviet forces opposite of Army Group South, codenamed Case Blue. After breaking through Red Army forces by 13 July, German forces encircled and captured the city of Rostov. Following the fall of Rostov, Hitler split German forces operating in the southern extremity of the southern Russian SFSR in an effort to simultaneously capture the city of Stalingrad and the Caucasus oil fields. The responsibility to take Stalingrad was given to the Sixth Army, which immediately turned towards the Volga River and began its advance with heavy air support from the *Luftwaffe's Luftflotte 4*. On 7 August, two German panzer corps were able to flank and encircle a Soviet force of 50,000 personnel and approximately 1,000 tanks, and on 22 August German forces began to cross the Don River to complete the advance towards the Volga. The following day, the Battle of Stalingrad began when vanguards of the Sixth Army penetrated the suburbs of the city.

By November the Sixth Army had occupied most of Stalingrad, pushing the defending Red Army to the banks of the Volga River. By this stage, there were indications of an impending Soviet offensive which would target Wehrmacht forces around the city, including increased Soviet activity opposite the Sixth Army's flanks, and information gained through the interrogation of Soviet prisoners. However, the German command was intent upon finalizing its capture of Stalingrad. In fact, head of Army General Staff General Franz Halder

Figure 16: *German troops advancing in the Soviet Union, June 1942*

had been dismissed in September after his efforts to warn about the danger which was developing along the over-extended flanks of the Sixth Army and the Fourth Panzer Army. As early as September the Soviet *Stavka* (high command) began planning a series of counteroffensives to encompass the destruction of German forces in the south, fighting in Stalingrad and in the Caucasus, and against Army Group Center. Ultimately, command of Soviet efforts to relieve Stalingrad was put under the leadership of General Aleksandr Vasilevsky.

The *Stavka* developed two major operations to be conducted against Axis forces near Stalingrad, *Uranus* and *Saturn*, and also planned for Operation *Mars*, designed to engage German Army Group Center in an effort to distract reinforcements and to inflict as much damage as possible. Operation *Uranus* involved the use of large Soviet mechanized and infantry forces to encircle German and other Axis forces directly around Stalingrad. As preparations for the offensive commenced, the attack's starting points were positioned on stretches of front to the rear of the German Sixth Army, largely preventing the Germans from reinforcing those sectors quickly where Axis units were too overstretched to occupy effectively. The offensive was a double envelopment; Soviet mechanized forces would penetrate deep into the German rear, while another attack would be made closer to the German Sixth Army in an effort to attack German units there directly in the rear. While the Red Army prepared, the German high commanders—influenced by their belief that the Red Army, building up opposite Germany Army Group Center to the north,

Figure 17: *General Friedrich Paulus, commander of the German Sixth Army*

was incapable of mounting a simultaneous offensive in the south—continued to deny the possibility of an impending Soviet offensive.

Comparison of forces

Axis

Case Blue involved German and other Axis forces sprawled out across a front over 480 kilometers (300 mi) wide and several hundred kilometers deep, while the decision to conquer Stalingrad had stretched Axis forces even more thinly by drawing away personnel eastwards. For example, in early July the Sixth Army was defending a 160-kilometer (99 mi) line, while also committing to an offensive which involved a distance of around 400 kilometers (250 mi). Army Group B, which was split from Army Group South (the forces operating around the Caucasus were named Army Group A), seemed strong on paper: it included the Second and Sixth German, Fourth *Panzer*, Fourth and Third Romanian, Eighth Italian, and Second Hungarian Armies. Army Group B had the 48th Panzer Corps, which had the strength of a weakened panzer division, and a single infantry division as reserves. For the most part the German flanks were held by arriving non-German Axis armies, while German forces were used to spearhead continued operations in Stalingrad and in the Caucasus.

While Adolf Hitler expressed confidence in the ability of non-German Axis units to protect German flanks, in reality these units relied on largely obsolete equipment and horse-drawn artillery, while in many cases the harsh treatment of enlisted personnel by officers caused poor morale. In regard to mechanization, the First Romanian Armored Division was equipped with around 100 Czech-built Panzer 35(t) tanks, armed with a 37-millimeter (1.5 in) gun ineffective against the armor of Soviet T-34 tanks. Similarly, their 37-millimeter (1.5 in) PaK anti-tank guns were also antiquated and they were largely short of ammunition. Only after repeated requests did the Germans send the Romanian units 75-millimeter (3.0 in) PaK guns; six per division. These units were extended over very large sections of front; for example, the Third Romanian Army occupied a line 140 kilometers (87 mi) long, while the Fourth Romanian Army protected a line no less than 270 kilometers (170 mi) long. The Italians and Hungarians were positioned at the Don west of the Third Romanian Army, but the German commanders did not hold in high regard the capability of those units to fight.

Generally, German forces were in no better shape; they were weakened by months of fighting the Red Army, and, while *Stavka* raised new armies, the German high command attempted to maintain its existing mechanized units. Furthermore, during the course of the German offensive between May and November 1942, two motorized divisions, the elite Leibstandarte and the Großdeutschland, were redeployed from Army Group A to the West, to provide a mechanized reserve in case of an Allied landing in France. The Sixth Army had also suffered many casualties during the fighting in the city of Stalingrad proper. In some cases, such as that of the 22nd Panzer Division, their equipment was no better than that of the First Romanian Armored Division. German formations were also overextended along large stretches of front; the XI Army Corps, for example, had to defend a front around 100 kilometers (62 mi) long.

Soviet

The Red Army allocated an estimated 1,100,000 personnel, 804 tanks, 13,400 artillery pieces and over 1,000 aircraft for the upcoming offensive. Across the Third Romanian Army, the Soviets placed the redeployed 5th Tank Army, as well as the 21st and 65th Armies, in order to penetrate and overrun the German flanks. The German southern flank was targeted by the Stalingrad Front's 51st and 57th Armies, led by the 13th and 4th Mechanized Corps; these would punch through the Fourth Romanian Army, in order to link up with the 5th Tank Army near the town of Kalach. In total, the Soviets had amassed 11 armies and various independent tank brigades and corps.

Preparations for the offensive were, however, far from perfect; on 8 November, *Stavka* issued orders to postpone the launch date of the operation, because transportation delays had prevented many units from being able to move into place. In the meantime, units at the front went through a number of war games to practice repelling an enemy counterattack and exploiting a breakthrough with mechanized forces. These movements were masked through a deception campaign by the Soviets, including the decrease of radio traffic, camouflage, operational security, using couriers for communication instead of radio, and active deception, such as increasing troop movements around Moscow. Troops were ordered to build defensive fortifications, to offer false impressions to the Germans, while fake bridges were put up to divert attention from the real bridges being built across the Don River. The Red Army also stepped up attacks against Army Group Center and set up dummy formations to maintain the idea of a main offensive against German forces in the center.

The Soviet Stalingrad Front forces were subject to heavy bombardment, making mobilization more difficult. The 38 engineer battalions allocated to the front were responsible for ferrying ammunition, personnel and tanks across the Volga River while carrying out minor reconnaissance along sections of the front which were to be the breakthrough points of the impending offensive. In three weeks the Red Army transported around 111,000 soldiers, 420 tanks and 556 artillery pieces across the Volga.

On 17 November Vasilevsky was recalled to Moscow, where he was shown a letter written to Stalin by General Volsky, commander of the 4th Mechanized Corps, who urged calling off the offensive. Volsky believed the offensive as planned was doomed to failure due to the state of the forces earmarked for the operation; he suggested postponing the offensive and redesigning it entirely. Many Soviet soldiers had not been issued with winter garments, and many died of frostbite, "due to the irresponsible attitude of commanders". Although Soviet intelligence made honest efforts to collect as much information as possible on the disposition of the Axis forces arrayed in front of them, there was not much information on the state of the German Sixth Army. The Soviet commanders, overruling Vasilevsky, agreed the offensive would not be called off, and Stalin personally rang Volsky, who reiterated his intention to carry out the operation if ordered to do so.

Soviet offensive

Operation *Uranus*, postponed until 17 November, was again postponed for two days when Soviet General Georgy Zhukov was told the air units allotted to the operation were not ready; it was finally launched on 19 November. Shortly after 5 a.m. Lieutenant Gerhard Stöck, posted with the Romanian IV Army Corps on the Kletskaya sector called Sixth Army headquarters

Figure 18: *Romanian soldier on the front*

housed in Golubinsky, offering intelligence on a pending attack which would occur after 05:00 that morning; however, because his call had come in after five and false alarms were common during this time, the duty officer on the other end of the line was not keen on waking the Army Chief of Staff, General Arthur Schmidt. Although Soviet commanders suggested postponing the bombardment due to poor visibility due to thick fog, front headquarters decided to proceed. At 07:20 Moscow time (05:20 German time) Soviet artillery commanders received the codeword "Siren", prompting an 80-minute artillery bombardment directed almost entirely against the non-German Axis units protecting the German flanks. At 7:30, the Katyusha rocket-launchers fired the first salvos and were soon joined in by the 3,500 guns and mortars stretching along the few breakthrough sectors in front of the Third Romanian Army and the northern shoulder of the German Sixth Army's flank. Although thick fog prevented the Soviet artillery from correcting their aim, their weeks of preparation and ranging allowed them to lay down accurate fire on enemy positions along the front. The effect was devastating, as communication lines were breached, ammunition dumps destroyed and forward observation points shattered. Many Romanian personnel who survived the bombardment began to flee to the rear. Soviet heavy artillery aimed at Romanian artillery positions and second-echelon formations also caught the retreating Romanian soldiers.

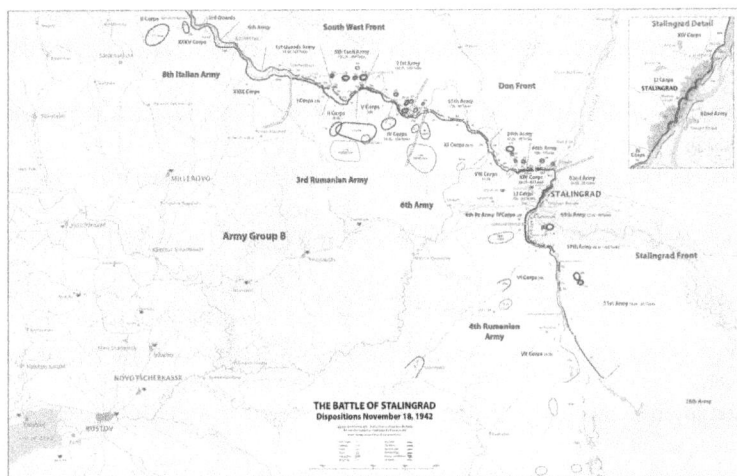

Figure 19: *Unit locations of Axis and Soviet Armies on Nov 18, 1942.*

Against the Third Romanian Army: 19 November

The offensive against the Third Romanian Army began at 08:50, led by the 21st and 65th Soviet Armies and the 5th Tank Army. The first two assaults were repulsed by the Romanian defenders, and the effects of the heavy artillery bombardment had actually made it more difficult for Soviet armor to navigate through the minefields and terrain. However, the lack of heavy anti-tank artillery caused the Romanian defense to collapse; a breakthrough by the 4th Tank Corps and 3rd Guards Cavalry Corps was established by noon. Soon after, the 5th Tank Army was able to gain a breakthrough against the Second Romanian Corps, followed by the Eighth Cavalry Corps. As Soviet armor navigated through the thick fog by compass, overrunning Romanian and German artillery positions, three Romanian infantry divisions began to fall back in disarray; the Third Romanian Army had been outflanked to the West and East. After receiving the news of the Soviet attack, Sixth Army headquarters failed to order the 16th and 24th Panzer Divisions, hitherto engaged in Stalingrad, to reorient themselves to bolster the Romanian defenses; instead the task was given to the seriously understrength and poorly equipped 48th Panzer Corps.

The 48th Panzer Corps had fewer than 100 serviceable modern tanks to combat Soviet armor. Furthermore, they lacked fuel, and the shortage of tanks forced commanders to organize tank crews into infantry companies; the 22nd Panzer Division, which formed part of the corps, was almost completely destroyed in the fighting that ensued. The 22nd had entered the fighting with fewer than thirty working tanks, and left with a company of tanks. The Romanian 1st Armored Division, attached to the 48th Panzer Corps, engaged the Soviet 26th Tank Corps after having lost communications with their German corps commanders, and were defeated by 20 November. As the Soviets continued to advance southwards, many Soviet tank crews began to suffer from the worsening blizzard, which affected men and equipment, and blocked gunsights. It was not uncommon for tanks to lose traction on the ground, and for a crew member to have an arm broken as he was thrown around inside the hull. However, the blizzard also neutralized the German corps' coordination.

The rout of the Third Romanian Army began by the end of 19 November. The Soviet 21st Army and 5th Tank Army were able to capture some 27,000 Romanian prisoners—the bulk of three divisions—and then continue their advance southwards. Soviet cavalry was used to exploit the breakthrough, sever communications between the Romanians and the Italian 8th Army, and to block any possible counterattack against the Soviet flank. While the Red Air Force strafed retreating Romanian soldiers, the *Luftwaffe* provided only negligible opposition. The withdrawal of the 1st Romanian Cavalry Division, originally positioned on the German 376th Infantry Division's flank, allowed the 65th Army to bypass German defenses. As German forces began to react late on 19 November, another attack developed on the Sixth Army's flank to the south.

Against the German southern flank: 20 November

In the early morning of 20 November *Stavka* telephoned Stalingrad Front commander Andrei Yeremenko asking if he would begin his portion of the offensive on schedule, at 08:00. He responded he would do so only if the fog lifted; although the 51st Army opened its artillery barrage on time because front headquarters could not contact the division, the rest of the forces prepared for the operation received orders to postpone the attack until 10:00. The 51st Army engaged the Romanian 6th Corps, taking many prisoners. As the 57th Army joined the attack at 10:00, the situation developed in such a way that the Stalingrad Front could throw its armored corps into battle. The German 297th Infantry Division watched as its Romanian support failed to put up resistance against the Red Army. However, confusion and lack of control caused the Soviet 4th and 13th Mechanized Corps to stumble as they began to exploit the breakthroughs achieved by the opening offensive.

The Germans responded quickly by redeploying their only reserve in the area, the 29th Panzergrenadier Division. Despite initial victories against Soviet armored forces, the Romanian collapse forced the division to again redeploy in an attempt to shore up defenses to the south. The 29th Panzergrenadier Division's counterattack had cost the Red Army around fifty tanks, and caused Soviet commanders to worry about the safety of their left flank. However, the

Figure 20: *Panzer III in the southern Soviet Union, December 1942*

German division's redeployment meant that by the end of the day only the 6th Romanian Cavalry Regiment was positioned between advancing Soviet forces and the Don River.

Continued operations: 20–23 November

While the Stalingrad Front launched its offensive on 20 November, the 65th Soviet Army continued to apply pressure to the German 11th Corps along the northern shoulder of the Sixth Army's flank. The Red Army's 4th Tank Corps advanced beyond the German 11th Corps, while the 3rd Guards Cavalry Corps crashed into the German unit's rear. The German 376th Infantry Division and the Austrian 44th Infantry Division began to redeploy to face the enemy on their flanks, but were hindered by shortage of fuel. The 14th Panzer Division's remaining panzer regiment destroyed a flanking regiment of the Soviet 3rd Guards Cavalry Corps, but its anti-tank artillery suffered heavy casualties when it was overrun by Soviet forces. By the end of the day the Soviet 1st Tank Corps was chasing the retreating 48th Panzer Corps, while the Soviet 26th Tank Corps had captured the town of Perelazovsky, almost 130 kilometers (81 mi) to the northwest of Stalingrad.

The Red Army's offensive continued on 21 November, with forces of the Stalingrad Front achieving penetrations of up to 50 kilometers (31 mi). By this time remaining Romanian units in the north were being destroyed in isolated

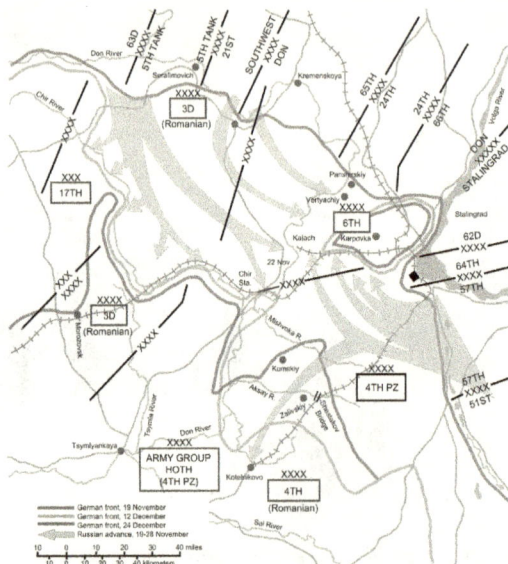

battles, while the Red Army began to engage flanking portions of the German Fourth Panzer and Sixth Armies. The German 22nd Panzer Division, despite attempting a short counterattack, was reduced to little more than a tank company and forced to withdraw to the southwest. The Soviet 26th Tank Corps, having destroyed a large portion of the Romanian 1st Armored Division, continued its advance to the southeast, avoiding engaging enemy left behind, although remnants of the Romanian 5th Corps were able to reorganize and put up a hastily constructed defense in the hope that it would be aided by the German 48th Panzer Corps. Surrounded by 5th Tank Army on one side and 21st Army on the other, the bulk of 3rd Romanian Army was isolated in the region of Raspopinskaya where General Lascar took control of the remnants of 4th and 5th Corps, whereas the neighboring 1st Armored Division was still trying to break free and link with 22nd Panzer Division. That day German General Friedrich Paulus, commander of the Sixth Army, received reports that the Soviets were less than 40 kilometers (25 mi) from his headquarters; furthermore, there were no remaining units which could contest the Soviet advance. In the south, after a brief halt, the Soviet 4th Mechanized Corps continued its advance north, removing German defenders from several towns in the area, towards Stalingrad. As German forces in and around Stalingrad were at risk, Hitler ordered German forces in the area to establish an "all-around defensive position" and designated forces between the Don and Volga rivers as "Fortress Stalingrad", rather than allow the Sixth Army to attempt to break out. The Sixth Army, other Axis units, and most of the Fourth Panzer Army's German units were caught inside the growing Soviet encirclement. Only the 16th Panz-ergrenadier Division began to fight its way out. Lack of coordination between Soviet tanks and infantry as the Red Army's tank corps attempted to exploit the breakthrough along the Germans' southern flank allowed much of the Fourth Romanian Army to escape destruction.

On 22 November Soviet forces began to cross the Don River and continued their advance towards the town of Kalach. German forces defending Kalach, mostly composed of maintenance and supply personnel, were not aware of the Soviet offensive until 21 November, and even then did not know in what strength the Red Army was approaching. The task of taking the bridge at Kalach was given to the Soviet 26th Tank Corps, which used two captured Ger-man tanks and a reconnaissance vehicle to approach it and fire on the guards. Soviet forces broke into the town by mid-morning and drove the defenders out, allowing themselves and the 4th Tank Corps to link up with the Red Army's 4th Mechanized Corps approaching from the south. The encirclement of German forces in Stalingrad was completed on 22 November 1942. That day Soviet formations also continued to fight pockets of Romanian resistance, such as that put up by the Romanian 5th Corps.

The encirclement of 6th Army was effective on 23 November. Around 16:00, near the village of Sovetsky, the forward detachments of 36th Mechanized Brigade from the Stalingrad Front's 4th Mechanized Corps sighted the ap-proaching tanks of 45th Brigade from the Southwestern Front's 4th Tank Corps. At first they mistook them for Germans because they did not fire green flares as was agreed for a reconnaissance signal and several tanks were dam-aged in a short exchange of fire. After clarification the linkup was achieved. It was reenacted later for the newsreels.

The junction between the armored troops of 21st and 51st Armies from Vatutin's and Eremenko's fronts completed the surrounding of Paulus's group of forces: two German armies among the most powerful in the Wehrmacht, 22 divisions and 150 separate regiments or battalions, and an enormous amount of materiel. Never before in the war were so many troops of the mighty Ger-many caught together. Such a feat was so unusual that the Stavka's own ini-tial estimation of the encircled enemy force was only a quarter of its actual strength, because besides the fighting troops there was a huge amount of extra personnel from various professions, engineer sections, Luftwaffe ground staff and others. Fighting continued on 23 November as the Germans attempted in vain to mount local counterattacks to break the encirclement. By this time Axis personnel inside the encirclement moved east towards Stalingrad to avoid Soviet tanks, while those that managed to escape the encirclement moved west toward German and other Axis forces.

Aftermath

Operation *Uranus* trapped between 250,000 and 300,000 Axis soldiers within an area stretching 50 kilometers (31 mi) from east to west and 40 kilometers (25 mi) north to south. The pocket contained four infantry corps, a panzer corps belonging to the Fourth Panzer and Sixth Armies, and surviving elements of two Romanian divisions, a Croat infantry regiment and other specialist units. Trapped equipment included around 100 tanks, 2,000 artillery pieces and mortars and 10,000 trucks. The withdrawal to Stalingrad left lines of retreat littered with helmets, weapons and other equipment, and heavy equipment which had been destroyed was left on the side of the road. Bridges spanning the Don River were jammed with traffic, as surviving Axis soldiers hastily made their way eastwards in the cold weather, attempting to escape Soviet armor and infantry threatening to cut them off from Stalingrad. Many wounded Axis personnel were trampled, and many of those who attempted to cross the river on foot on the ice fell through and drowned. Hungry soldiers filled Russian villages scouring for supplies, while supply dumps were often looted in search of cans of food. The last stragglers crossed the Don River by 24 November, and demolished the bridges to seal off the Fourth Panzer and Sixth Armies from the Soviets in Stalingrad.

The Sixth Army, in the midst of chaos, began to build defensive lines, hampered by the lack of fuel, ammunition and rations, and further burdened by the advancing Russian winter. It was also tasked with plugging gaps in the line caused by the disintegrating Romanian forces. On 23 November, some German units destroyed or burned everything not necessary for a breakout operation and began to pull back towards the northern end of Stalingrad. However, after the Germans had abandoned their winter bunkers, the Soviet 62nd Army was able to destroy the German 94th Infantry Division on the open ground; survivors of the German division were attached to the 16th and 24th Panzer Divisions. Although German military commanders were of the opinion that Wehrmacht forces caught in the encirclement should break out, between 23 and 24 November Hitler decided instead to hold the position and attempt to resupply the Sixth Army by air. The personnel trapped in Stalingrad would require at least 680 metric tons (750 short tons) of supplies per day, a task which the depleted *Luftwaffe* was in no condition to carry out. Furthermore, the revived Red Air Force was a threat to German aircraft attempting to fly over the encirclement. Although by December the *Luftwaffe* had assembled a fleet of around 500 aircraft, this was still insufficient to supply the Sixth Army and elements of the Fourth Panzer Army with the required supplies. During the first half of December the Sixth Army received less than 20% of their daily requirements.

In the meantime, the Red Army strengthened its outer encirclement with the intention of destroying the encircled German units. Soviet armies would attack German units to the east and the south, aiming to split German units into smaller groups. These orders became effective on 24 November, and were to be executed without a major regrouping or movement of reserves. The outer encirclement ran for an estimated 320 kilometers (200 mi), although only three-quarters of that distance was actually covered by Soviet troops; the distance between the outer and inner encirclements was around 16 kilometers (9.9 mi). The Soviet high command also began planning for Operation *Saturn*, which was aimed at destroying the Italian Eighth Army and cutting off German forces in the Caucasus. The Soviet *Stavka* planned *Saturn* to start on about 10 December.

German forces in the area had been further split up, as German general Erich von Manstein was given command of the newly created Army Group Don, comprising the German Fourth Panzer and Sixth Armies, and the Third and Fourth Romanian Armies. Although the situation looked bleak for the Germans, a moment of relative calm had settled after the end of Operation *Uranus*; German and Soviet forces were planning their next movements.

References

<templatestyles src=”Template:Refbegin/styles.css” />

- Beevor, Antony (1998). *Stalingrad: The Fateful Siege: 1942 – 1943*. Harmondsworth, United Kingdom: Penguin Putnam Inc. ISBN 0-670-87095-1.
- Bell, Kelly (Fall 2006). ”Struggle for Stalin's Skies”. *WWII History: Russian Front*. Special. Herndon, Virginia: Sovereign Media. Issue. 1539-5456.
- Bergström, Christer (2007). *Stalingrad – The Air Battle: 1942 through January 1943*. Harmondsworth, United Kingdom: Chevron Publishing Limited. ISBN 978-1-85780-276-4.
- Clark, Alan (1965). *Barbarossa: The Russian-German Conflict, 1941–1945*. New York City, New York: William Morrow. ISBN 0-688-04268-6.
- Cooper, Matthew (1978). *The German Army 1933–1945*. Lanham, Maryland: Scarborough House. ISBN 0-8128-8519-8.
- Erickson, John (1983). *The Road to Berlin: Stalin's War with Germany*. Yale University Press. ISBN 0-300-07813-7.
- Erickson, John (1975). *The Road to Stalingrad: Stalin's War With Germany*. Yale University Press. ISBN 0-300-07812-9.

- Glantz, David M. (January 1996). "Soviet Military Strategy During the Second Period of War (November 1942 – December 1943): A Reappraisal". *The Journal of Military History*. Society for Military History. **60** (1): 35. doi: 10.2307/2944451[115].

- Glantz, David M.; House, Jonathan (1995). *When Titans Clashed: How the Red Army Stopped Hitler*. Lawrence, Kansas: Kansas University Press. ISBN 0-7006-0717-X.

- Glantz, David M. (1999). *Zhukov's Greatest Defeat: The Red Army's Epic Disaster in Operation Mars, 1942*. Lawrence, Kansas: Kansas University Press. ISBN 0-7006-0944-X.

- Joly, Anton (2014). *Stalingrad Battle Atlas, Volume III*. Paris, France: Staldata Publications. ISBN 979-10-93222-06-6.

- McCarthy, Peter; Syron, Mike (2002). *Panzerkrieg: The Rise and Fall of Hitler's Tank Divisions*. New York City, New York: Carroll & Graf. ISBN 0-7867-1009-8.

- McTaggart, Pat (Fall 2006). "Soviet Circle of Iron". *WWII History: Russian Front*. Special. Herndon, Virginia: Sovereign Media. Issue. 1539-5456.

- Perrett, Bryan (1998). *German Light Panzers 1932–42*. Oxford, United Kingdom: Osprey. ISBN 1-85532-844-5.

- von Manstein, Erich (1982). *Lost Victories*. St. Paul, MN: Zenith Press. ISBN 0891411305.

External links

Wikimedia Commons has media related to *Operation Uranus*.

- Order of Battle for operation Uranus[116]

<indicator name="featured-star"> ⭐ </indicator>

End of the battle

Operation Winter Storm

Operation *Winter Storm*	
Part of Battle of Stalingrad, Eastern Front, World War II	

A German Tiger tank and knocked-out Soviet T-34 tank during the fighting in the southern Soviet Union.

Date	12–23 December 1942
Location	Southwest of Stalingrad
Result	Soviet victory • Axis failure to rescue 6th Army in Stalingrad pocket

Belligerents	
Soviet Union	Germany Romania Italy

Commanders and leaders	
Aleksandr Vasilevsky	Erich von Manstein Hermann Hoth Petre Dumitrescu Italo Gariboldi

Strength	
150,000 personnel 630 tanks 1,500 artillery guns[117]	est. 50,000[118] personnel 250 tanks[119]

Casualties and losses	
Unknown	**From 11 to 31 December 1942**: 15,751 casualties (3,700 killed, 10,874 wounded and 1,086 missing)

Operation *Winter Storm* (German: *Unternehmen Wintergewitter*) was a German offensive in World War II in which the German 4th Panzer Army unsuccessfully attempted to break the Soviet encirclement of the German 6th Army during the Battle of Stalingrad.

In late November 1942, the Red Army completed Operation Uranus, encircling some 300,000 Axis personnel in and around the city of Stalingrad. German forces within the Stalingrad pocket and directly outside were reorganized under Army Group Don, under the command of Field Marshal Erich von Manstein. Meanwhile, the Red Army continued to allocate as many resources as possible to the eventual launch of the planned Operation Saturn, which aimed to isolate Army Group A from the rest of the German Army. To remedy the situation, the *Luftwaffe* attempted to supply German forces in Stalingrad through an air bridge. When the *Luftwaffe* proved incapable of carrying out its mission and it became obvious that a successful breakout could occur only if launched as early as possible, Manstein decided on a relief effort.

Originally, Manstein was promised four *panzer* divisions. Due to German reluctance to weaken certain sectors by redeploying German units, the task of opening a corridor to the German 6th Army fell to the 4th Panzer Army. The German force was pitted against several Soviet armies tasked with the destruction of the encircled German forces and their offensive around the lower Chir River.

The German offensive caught the Red Army by surprise and made large gains on the first day. The spearhead forces enjoyed air support and were able to defeat counterattacks by Soviet troops. By 13 December, Soviet resistance slowed the German advance considerably. Although German forces took the area surrounding Verkhne-Kumskiy, the Red Army launched Operation Little Saturn on 16 December. Operation Little Saturn crushed the Italian 8th Army on Army Group Don's left flank, threatening the survival of Manstein's entire group of forces. As resistance and casualties increased, Manstein appealed to Hitler and to the commander of the German 6th Army, General Friedrich Paulus, to allow the 6th Army to break out of Stalingrad; both refused. The 4th Panzer Army continued its attempt to open a corridor to the 6th Army on 18–19 December, but was unable to do so without the aid of forces inside the Stalingrad pocket. Manstein called off the assault on 23 December and by Christmas Eve the 4th Panzer Army began to withdraw to its starting position. Due to the failure of the 6th Army to break out from the Soviet encirclement, the Red Army was able to continue the strangulation of German forces in Stalingrad.

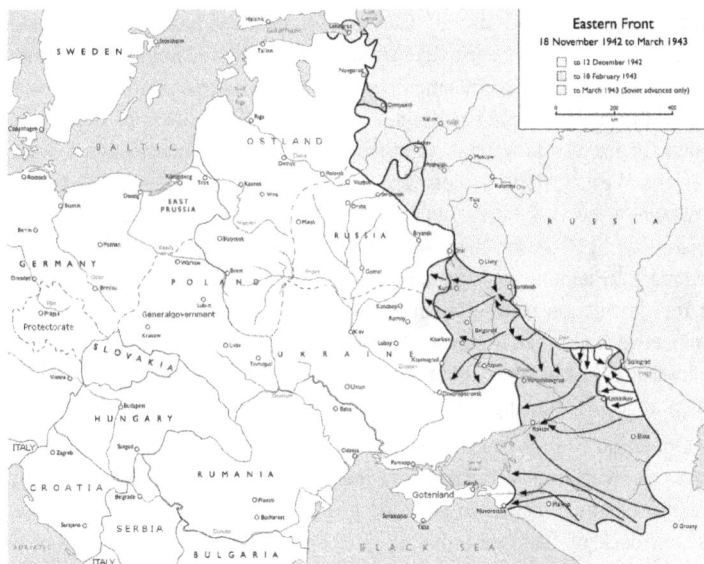

Figure 21: *The Eastern Front between 19 November 1942 and 1 March 1943*

Background

On 23 November 1942, the Red Army closed its encirclement of Axis forces in Stalingrad.[120] Nearly 300,000 German and Romanian soldiers, as well as Russian volunteers for the *Wehrmacht*, were trapped in and around the city of Stalingrad[121] by roughly 1.1 million Soviet personnel.[122] Amidst the impending disaster, German chancellor Adolf Hitler appointed Field Marshal Erich von Manstein as commander of the newly created Army Group Don.[123] Composed of the German 4th Panzer and 6th Armies, as well as the Third and Fourth Romanian Armies, Manstein's new army group was situated between German Army Groups A and B.[124] Instead of attempting an immediate breakout, German high command decided that the trapped forces would remain in Stalingrad in a bid to hold out.[125] The encircled German forces were to be resupplied by air, requiring roughly 680 t (750 short tons) of supplies per day. However, the assembled fleet of 500 transport aircraft were insufficient for the task.[126] Many of the aircraft were hardly serviceable in the rough Soviet winter; in early December, more German cargo planes were destroyed in accidents than by Soviet fighter aircraft.[127] The German 6th Army, for example, was getting less than 20% of its daily needs.[128] Furthermore, the Germans were still threatened by Soviet forces which still held portions of the Volga River's west bank in Stalingrad.[129]

Given the unexpected size of German forces closed off in Stalingrad,[130] on 23 November *Stavka* (Soviet Armed Forces High Command) decided to strengthen the outer encirclement preparing to destroy Axis forces in and around the city.[131] On 24 November, several Soviet formations began to entrench themselves to defend against possible German incursions originating from the West.[132] The Soviets also reinforced the encircling forces in order to prevent a successful breakout operation by the German 6th Army and other Axis units.[133] However, this tied down over ½ of the Red Army's strength in the area.[134] Planning for Operation Saturn began on 25 November,[135] aiming for the destruction of the Italian 8th Army and the severing of communications between German forces west of the Don River and those operating in the Caucasus.[136] Meanwhile, planning also began for Operation Koltso (Ring), which aimed at reducing German forces in the Stalingrad pocket.[137]

As Operation Uranus concluded, German forces inside the encirclement were too weak to attempt a breakout on their own. Half of their remaining armor, for example, had been lost during the defensive fighting, and there was a severe lack of fuel and ammunition for the surviving vehicles, given that the *Luftwaffe* was not able to provide adequate aerial resupply.[138] Manstein proposed a counterstrike to break the Soviet encirclement of Stalingrad, codenamed Operation Winter Storm (German: *Wintergewitter*).[139] Manstein believed that—due to the inability of the *Luftwaffe* to supply the Stalingrad pocket—it was becoming more important to relieve them "at the earliest possible date".[140] On 28 November, Manstein sent Hitler a detailed report on Army Group Don's situation, including the strength of the German 6th Army and an assessment on the available ammunition for German artillery inside the city.[141] The dire strategic situation made Manstein doubtful on whether or not the relief operation could afford to wait to receive all units earmarked for the offensive.[142]

Stavka postponed Operation Saturn until 16 December, as Soviet forces struggled to clear German defenders from the lower Chir River. The Red Army's offensive in the area commenced on 30 November, involving around 50,000 soldiers, which forced Manstein to use the 48th Panzer Corps in an attempt to hold the area.[143] In response, the 5th Tank Army was reinforced by the newly created 5th Shock Army, drawn from existing formations of the South-Western and Stalingrad Fronts; the 5th Tank Army totaled nearly 71,000 men, 252 tanks and 814 artillery guns.[144] The Soviet offensive succeeded in tying down the 48th Panzer Corps, originally chosen to lead one of the main attacks on the Soviet encirclement.[145] The Soviets were forewarned of the impending German assault when they discovered the German 6th Panzer Division unloading at the town of Morozovsk, and as a result, held back several armies from the attack on the lower Chir River to prepare for a possible breakout attempt by German forces inside Stalingrad.[146]

Figure 22: *Field Marshal Erich von Manstein, commander of Army Group Don at the time of the battle*

Comparison of forces

Participating German forces

The relief operation was originally scheduled to include the LVII Panzer Corps of the 4th Panzer Army, under the command of General Friedrich Kirchner, including the 6th and 23rd Panzer Divisions, and Army Detachment Hollidt, consisting of three infantry divisions and two armored divisions (11th and 22nd Panzer Divisions).[147] In total, it was expected that four *panzer* divisions, four infantry divisions and three Luftwaffe Field Divisions were to take part in Operation Winter Storm. They would be tasked with temporarily opening a passage to the 6th Army.[148] The *Luftwaffe* field divisions—formed of non-combat soldiers, headquarters staffs and unit-less *Luftwaffe* and *Heer* personnel—were poorly trained and lacked seasoned officers and enlisted soldiers, as well as sufficient anti-tank and artillery guns.[149] Many of the personnel promised for the relief effort never arrived, partly due to the poor transportation service to the front, while some units originally chosen to be transferred under the command of Army Group Don were retained by their original commands.[150] Other units in Army Group Don were in no shape to conduct offensive operations, due to losses sustained in the past month of combat, while many new formations which had been promised did not arrive on time.[151]

On the other hand, the 11th Panzer Division was one of the most complete German armored divisions on the Eastern Front since it had just been transferred out of the German Army's reserve. The 6th Panzer Division was also complete because it had been transferred to Manstein's control from Western Europe.[152] However, the usefulness of the 11th Panzer Division was compromised when the Soviets launched their offensive against forces in the lower Chir River area, as this tied Army Detachment Hollidt down on the defensive.[153] Because of this, and because Manstein believed that a thrust originating from the position of Army Detachment Hollidt would be too obvious, the German field marshal decided to use the 4th Panzer Army and the XLVIII Panzer Corps as the main components of the relief operation.[154] However, despite attempts by the Germans to build strength for the offensive, their position along the lower Chir River became tenuous;[155] the Soviet breakthrough was only blunted by the arrival of the 11th Panzer Division, which was able to destroy the bulk of two Soviet tank brigades.[156] Consequently, the XLVIII Panzer Corps became embroiled in the defensive battles for the Chir River, as the Soviets pushed in an attempt to overrun the airfield at Tatsinskaya (being used to resupply German forces in Stalingrad by air).[157]

Although the LVII Panzer Corps was reluctantly released to Army Group Don, by Army Group A, the 17th Panzer Division was ordered back to its original area of concentration, and did not prepare to go back to Army Group Don until 10 days after it had been asked for.[158] In light of the troubles in building up sufficient forces, and seeing that the Soviets were concentrating more mechanization on the Chir River, Manstein decided to launch Operation Winter Storm using the 4th Panzer Army. Manstein hoped that the 6th Army would launch an offensive of its own, from the opposite side, upon the receipt of the code signal Thunderclap.[159:137] Manstein was gambling on Hitler accepting that the only plausible method to avoid the demise of the 6th Army was allowing it to break out, and assumed that General Paulus would agree to order his forces to escape the Stalingrad pocket.[160] On 10 December, Manstein communicated to Paulus that the relief operation would commence in 24 hours.[161]

Participating Soviet forces

For the purpose of Operation Uranus, Soviet Marshal Georgy Zhukov deployed eleven Soviet armies.[162] In an effort to bolster the offensive capabilities of the Stalingrad Front, over 420 tanks, 111,000 soldiers and 556 artillery guns were shipped over the Volga River in a period of three weeks.[163] The Red Army and Red Air Force were able to amass over one million soldiers, 13,500 artillery guns, 890 tanks and 1,100 combat aircraft, organized into 66 rifle divisions, five tank corps, 14 tank brigades, a single mechanized brigade, a cavalry corps, and 127 artillery and mortar regiments.[164] As the encirclement closed and the

Bundesarchiv, Bild I011-457-0058-12
Foto: Kamm, Richard I 1942

Figure 23: *A battalion of Tiger I tanks was deployed to Army Group
Don in an effort to strengthen the German drive to Stalingrad.*

Soviets continued with secondary operations, the 51st Army was positioned
on the edge of the outer encirclement with 34,000 men and 77 tanks. South
of them was the 28th Army, with 44,000 soldiers, 40 tanks and 707 artillery
guns and mortars. Concurrently, the Red Army began building its strength for
Operation Saturn, in which it would aim to isolate and destroy German Army
Group A in the Caucasus.[165]

German offensive

On 12 December 1942, Hoth's Fourth Panzer Army's LVII Panzer Corps began its north-eastward drive toward German forces trapped in the Stalingrad
pocket.[166] The 6th and 23rd Panzer Divisions made large gains, surprising the
Red Army and threatening the rear of the Soviet 51st Army. The German drive
was due to be spearheaded by the 503rd heavy tank battalion (Germany) of
Tiger I heavy tanks, but the unit did not embark on its transport to the Eastern
Front until December 21, 1942 and did not see battle until the very first days
of January 1943 along the Manytsch River. Initial progress of the Winterstorm
offensive was rapid. Some units were able to travel up to 50 km (31 mi) in the
first day.[167] The Germans were aided by the element of surprise, as *Stavka* had
not expected the German offensive to begin so soon, while General Vasilevsky
was unable to detach the 2nd Guards Army to use it as a blocking force against

Manstein's spearheads.[168] The initial advance had been so quick that the 6th Panzer Division was able to capture Soviet artillery equipment intact. Soviet resistance decreased noticeably after the 6th and 23rd Panzer Divisions had overrun the main body of Russian infantry.[169] In fact, the 302nd Rifle Division of the 51st Army was overrun by the end of 12 December.[170] Although Soviet infantry quickly reinforced villages in the path of the German drive, the Red Army's cavalry in the area was exhausted from weeks of combat and was incapable of putting up serious resistance against the German offensive.[171] Despite early gains, the LVII Panzer Corps was unable to achieve decisive results.[172] There were also reports of heavy pressure building against the 23rd Panzer Division, despite headway made on the first day of the German offensive.[173]

On 13 December, the 6th Panzer Division made contact with the Soviet 5th Tank Army,[174] which was engaged in the reduction of German defenses around the Chir River. German forces were able to engage and defeat Soviet armor,[175] as the former forced the crossing of the Alksay River.[176] At this point, a major armored battle began around the village of Verkhne-Kumskiy.[177]

The fate of the campaign was largely decided in this little Cossack village. Located on the most convenient south-north road to Stalingrad, whereas the barren steppe around was riddled with ravines and gullies covered with deep treacherous snow, Verkhne-Kumskiy was unavoidable for large armored forces to move north towards the Myshkova River.[178] On the Soviet side, Volsky's 4th Mechanized Corps was also driving at full speed towards the village. The corps had not yet had time to replenish personnel and material after the November offensive battles, it barely fielded 100 operable tanks, another 50 were in need of repair. Half of them were T-34 capable to oppose panzers Mk III and IV, the rest were light T-70, only useful against infantry or armored cars.[179] And yet this rather small force was the reason why the German relief operation failed. At this time the road towards the encircled 6th Army was almost, and if the 4th Mechanized Corps had not interfered, Hoth would have had a greater chance to reach Paulus.

Although they sustained heavy losses, the Soviet forces were able to push German forces back to the banks of the Alksay River by the end of the day, while failing to retake the town. However, the losses sustained by the Red Army in the vicinity of Verkhne-Kumskiy allowed the 6th Panzer Division to enjoy a brief superiority in tank numbers thereafter.[180] Fighting for Verkhne-Kumskiy continued for three days, as the Red Army launched a series of counterattacks against the German bridgeheads across the Alksay River and German defenders in the town.[181] German defenders were able to pin Soviet tanks in Verkhne-Kumskiy and destroy them using well emplaced anti-tank artillery guns.[182] With heavy support from the *Luftwaffe*, the Germans were able to

Figure 24: *German Panzer III in the Southern Soviet Union in December 1942*

achieve a local success and began to push toward the Myshkova river.[183] The 6th Panzer Division took heavy losses during its drive, and took a brief respite after the battle to recondition. Minor damage to surviving tanks was repaired and the majority of the tanks incapacitated during the fighting at Verkhne-Kumskiy were brought back to serviceable conditions.[184]

Soviet response: 13–18 December

The Fourth Panzer Army's offensive forced *Stavka* to recalculate its intentions for Operation Saturn, and on 13 December Stalin and *Stavka* authorized the redeployment of the 2nd Guards Army from the Don Front to the Stalingrad Front, where it would be ready to be used against German forces on 15 December.[185] This army had a strength of roughly 90,000 soldiers, organized into three Guards Rifle Corps (the 1st, 13th and 2nd).[186] Operation Saturn was redesigned into Operation Little Saturn, which limited the scope of the attack to breaking through the Italian 8th Army and then engaging Army Group Don in the rear.[187,188] The offensive was also changed from a southward push to a drive in a southeastern direction, and the start date was pushed back to 16 December.[189] In the meantime, the 4th Mechanized and 13th Tank Corps continued to counterattack against German forces in the vicinity of the Alksay River, trying to delay their advance in anticipation of the arrival of the 2nd Guards Army.[190]

The Soviet 1st and 3rd Guard Armies, in conjunction with the Soviet 6th Army, launched Operation Little Saturn on 16 December.[191] Despite early troubles due to stubborn resistance from Italian troops, the Red Army was able to partially overrun the Italian 8th Army by 18 December.[192] The breakthrough -even if small and quickly contained- proved a possible threat to Army Group Don's left flank, while the city of Rostov was threatened by the 3rd Guards Army.[193,194] This, and mainly heavy losses sustained by the German armor divisions forcing their way to the Myshkova river, forced Manstein to reconsider continuing the offensive.[195] The German field marshal decided that he could not defend his left flank while also sustaining the attempt to relieve the 6th Army.[196] Although the 6th Panzer Division was able to cross the Myshkova River by the night of 19 December,[197] the LVII Panzer Corps had still not made major advances against increased Soviet opposition, despite the arrival of the 17th Panzer Division; in fact, it seemed as if the corps would have to go on the defensive.[198] Furthermore, the Soviet raid on Tatsinskaya managed to destroy the airfield and several dozen aircraft being used by the *Luftwaffe* to resupply forces inside the Stalingrad pocket, forcing Manstein to order the XLVIII Panzer Corps on the defensive, instead of reserving it to bolster his forces directed toward the breakthrough to Stalingrad.[199] To make matters worse for the Germans, on 18 December Hitler refused to allow the German 6th Army to begin a breakout operation towards the rest of Army Group Don, despite pleas from Manstein.[200]

Collapse: 19–23 December

On 19 December, Manstein sent his chief intelligence officer—Major Eismann—into Stalingrad to give General Paulus an accurate image of the strategic situation which had befallen Army Group Don.[201] Paulus was not impressed, although he agreed that the best option continued to be an attempted breakout as early as possible.[202] The 6th Army's Chief of Staff—Major General Arthur Schmidt—argued that a breakout was unfeasible and instead suggested that Army Group Don take steps to better supply entrapped Axis forces by air.[203] Despite agreeing with Eismann earlier, Paulus then decided that a breakout was out of the question given the 6th Army's incapability to conduct it and Hitler's express orders against it.[204] Although that day the LVII Panzer Corps managed to break through the Alksay River and drive within 48 km (30 mi) of the southern edge of the 6th Army's front, the entrapped German forces made no attempt to link up with the relieving forces.[205] Adam makes the point the 6th Army tanks only had fuel to go 30 km, after which they would need fuel and ammunition flown in to go any further.:142–143 Thereafter, the 6th Army simply did not have the strength to attempt a breakout, operating less than 70 serviceable tanks, with limited supplies, while its infantry were in no condition to attempt an attack in the blizzard which had developed over the past few days.[206]

Manstein ordered the 6th Panzer Division to end its offensive and redeploy to the southern Chir River, to bolster German defenses there against the continuing Soviet offensive, on 23 December.[207] By 24 December, the Fourth Panzer Army was in full retreat,[153] returning to its starting position.[208] The inability to breakthrough to the 6th Army, and the latter formation's refusal to attempt a breakout, caused Operation Winter Storm to collapse on 24 December, as Army Group Don returned to the defensive.[209]

Aftermath

With the German relief effort defeated, *Stavka* was free to concentrate on the destruction of Axis forces in the Stalingrad pocket and the westward expansion of the Red Army's Winter offensive.[210] The Red Army was able to bring to bear almost 150,000 personnel and 630 tanks against the retreating 4th Panzer Army and although Volsky's 4th Mechanized Corps (renamed 3rd Guard Mechanized Corps on 18 December 1942) was withdrawn to be refitted, the 51st Army, the 1st Guards Rifle and 7th Tank Corps struck at German units withdrawing between the Mushkova and Aksai Rivers.[211] In three days, the attacking Soviet units broke through the Romanian positions guarding the LVII Panzer Corps' flank and threatened the 4th Panzer Army from the south, forcing the Germans to continue withdrawing to the southwest.[212] All the while, the XLVIII Panzer Corps—led mainly by the 11th Panzer Division—strove to maintain its position along the Chir River.[213] Despite success, the XLVIII Panzer Corps was rushed to the defense of Rostov as a Soviet breakthrough seemed imminent after the partial collapse of the Italian 8th Army.[214] As the Red Army pursued the 4th Panzer Army toward the Aksai River and broke through the German defense on the banks of the Chir River, it also began to prepare for Operation Ring—the reduction of the forces in Stalingrad.[215]

German forces in Stalingrad soon began to run out of supplies, with horse meat used to supplement diets.[216] By the end of 1942, the distance between the German 6th Army and forces outside of the encirclement was over 65 km (40 mi), and most of the German formations in the area were extremely weak.[217] Hitler's insistence in holding Stalingrad to the last risked the existence of the 6th Army.[218] The end of the German offensive also allowed the Red Army to continue in its efforts to cut off German forces in the Caucasus, which would begin in the middle of January.[219] On the other hand, the encirclement of the 6th Army and the operations to destroy it tied down a considerable number of Soviet troops, which affected Soviet operations on other sectors.[220]

Bibliography

<templatestyles src="Template:Refbegin/styles.css" />

- Beevor, Antony (1998). *Stalingrad: The Fateful Siege: 1942–1943*. Harmondsworth, United Kingdom: Penguin Putnam Inc. ISBN 0-670-87095-1.
- Bell, Kelly (Fall 2006). "Struggle for Stalin's Skies". *WWII History: Russian Front*. Special. Herndon, Virginia: Sovereign Media. Issue. 1539-5456.
- Clark, Alan (1965). *Barbarossa: The Russian-German Conflict, 1941–1945*. New York City, New York: William Morrow. ISBN 0-688-04268-6.
- Cooper, Matthew (1978). *The German Army 1933–1945*. Lanham, Maryland: Scarborough House. ISBN 0-8128-8519-8.
- Erickson, John (1983). *The Road to Berlin: Stalin's War with Germany*. New Haven, Connecticut: Yale University Press. ISBN 0-300-07813-7.
- Erickson, John (1975). *The Road to Stalingrad: Stalin's War With Germany*. New Haven, Connecticut: Yale University Press. ISBN 0-300-07812-9.
- Glantz, David M. (January 1996). "Soviet Military Strategy During the Second Period of War (November 1942 – December 1943): A Reappraisal". *The Journal of Military History*. Society for Military History. **60** (1): 35. doi: 10.2307/2944451[221]. JSTOR 2944451[222].
- Glantz, David M.; Jonathan House (1995). *When Titans Clashed: How the Red Army Stopped Hitler*. Lawrence, Kansas: Kansas University Press. ISBN 0-7006-0717-X.
- Heiber, Helmut; David M. Glantz (2003). *Hitler and his Generals: Military Conferences 1942–1945*. New York City, New York: Enigma Books. ISBN 1-929631-09-X.
- Isaev, A.B. (2008). <bdi lang="ru" >Сталинград. За Волгой для нас земли нет</bdi> (in Russian). Moscow, Russia: Exmo. ISBN 978-5-699-26236-6.
- McCarthy, Peter; Mike Syryon (2002). *Panzerkrieg: The Rise and Fall of Hitler's Tank Divisions*. New York City, New York: Carroll & Graf. ISBN 0-7867-1009-8.
- McTaggart, Pat (Fall 2006). "Soviet Circle of Iron". *WWII History: Russian Front*. Special. Herndon, Virginia: Sovereign Media. Issue. 1539-5456.
- Raus, Erhard (2002). *Panzers on the Eastern Front: General Erhard Raus and his Panzer Divisions in Russia 1941–1945*. Mechanicsburg, PA: Military Book Club. ISBN 0-7394-2644-3.

- von Manstein, Erich (1982). *Lost Victories*. St. Paul, MN: Zenith Press. ISBN 978-0-7603-2054-9.
- Joly, Anton (2017). *Stalingrad Battle Atlas, Volume IV, Operation Winter Storm*. Paris, France: Staldata Publications. ISBN 979-10-93222-09-7.

<indicator name="good-star"> ⊕ </indicator>

Operation Little Saturn

Operation Little Saturn	
Part of the Battle of Stalingrad during the Eastern Front	

Soviet advances during Operations Uranus, Mars and Saturn.

Date	12 December 1942 – 18 February 1943
Location	Northern Caucasus and the Donets Basin
Result	Soviet tactical victory

Belligerents	
🏴 Germany ▪ Italy ▪ Hungary ▪ Romania	▪ Soviet Union

Commanders and leaders	
🏴 Adolf Hitler 🏴 Erich von Manstein 🏴 Erhard Raus 🏴 Edwald von Kleist ▪ Italo Gariboldi ▪ Gusztáv Jány ▪ Petre Dumitrescu	▪ Joseph Stalin ▪ Fyodor Kuznetsov ▪ Dmitri Lelyushenko ▪ Vasyl Herasimenko ▪ Filipp Golikov

Operation Saturn, revised as **Operation Little Saturn**, was a Red Army operation on the Eastern Front of World War II that led to battles in the northern Caucasus and Donets Basin regions of the Soviet Union from December 1942 to February 1943.

The success of Operation Uranus, launched on 19 November 1942, had trapped 250,000–300,000 troops of General Friedrich Paulus' German 6th

Army and 4th Panzer Army in Stalingrad. To exploit this victory, the Soviet general staff planned a winter campaign of continuous and highly ambitious offensive operations, codenamed "Saturn". Later Joseph Stalin reduced his ambitious plans to a relatively small campaign codenamed "Operation Little Saturn". The offensive succeeded in smashing Germany's Italian and Hungarian allies, applied pressure on the over stretched German forces in Eastern Ukraine and prevented further German advances to the relief of the entrapped forces at Stalingrad. Despite these victories, the Soviets themselves became over extended, setting up the stages for the German offensives of the Third Battle of Kharkov and the Battle of Kursk.

Background

On 17 May 1942, German Army Groups A and B launched a counteroffensive against advancing Soviet armies around the city of Kharkov, resulting in the Second Battle of Kharkov;[223] this would ultimately be expanded on 28 June into Case Blue, which aimed the capture of the Caucasus oil fields.[224] By 6 July, General Hermann Hoth's Fourth Panzer Army had taken the city of Voronezh, threatening to collapse the Red Army's resistance.[225] By early August, General Paul Ludwig Ewald von Kleist's First Panzer Army had reached the oil center of Maykop, 500 kilometres (310 mi) south of the city of Rostov,[226] which had been taken by the Fourth Panzer Army on 23 July.[227] The rapid German advance threatened to cut the Soviet Union off from its southern territories, while also threatening to cut the lend-lease supply lines from Persia.[228] However, the offensive began to peter out, as the offensive's supply train struggled to keep up with the advance and spearhead units began to run low on fuel and manpower;[229] for example, some panzer divisions were down to 54 tanks.[230]

Operation Uranus

Operation Uranus was the codename of the Soviet strategic operation in World War II which led to the encirclement of the German Sixth Army, Third and Fourth Romanian armies, and portions of the German Fourth Panzer Army. The operation formed part of the ongoing Battle of Stalingrad, and was aimed at destroying German forces in and around Stalingrad. Planning for Operation *Uranus* had commenced as early as September 1942, and was developed simultaneously with plans to envelop and destroy German Army Group Center and German forces in the Caucasus. The Red Army took advantage of the fact that German forces in the southern Soviet Union were overstretched around Stalingrad, using weaker Romanian armies to guard their flanks; the offensive's starting points were established along the section of the front directly opposite

Romanian forces. These Axis armies were deployed in open positions on the steppe and lacked heavy equipment to deal with Soviet armor.

German attempt to relieve Stalingrad

Operation Winter Storm (*Unternehmen Wintergewitter*), undertaken between 12–23 December 1942, was the German Fourth Panzer Army's attempt to relieve encircled Axis forces during the Battle of Stalingrad. In late November, the Red Army completed Operation Uranus, which resulted in the encirclement of Axis personnel in and around the city of Stalingrad. German forces within the Stalingrad Pocket and directly outside were reorganized under Army Group Don, under the command of Field Marshal Erich von Manstein. As the Red Army continued to build strength, in an effort to allocate as many resources as possible to the eventual launch of the planned Operation Saturn, which aimed to isolate Army Group A from the rest of the German Army, the Luftwaffe had begun an attempt to supply German forces in Stalingrad through an air bridge. However, as the Luftwaffe proved incapable of carrying out its mission and it became more obvious that a successful breakout could only occur if it was launched as early as possible, Manstein decided to plan and launch a dedicated relief effort.

Soviet counter-offensive: Operation Little Saturn

After the defeat of the Romanian Army around Stalingrad and the successful encirclement of the German Sixth Army, Stalin started a counter-offensive nicknamed "Operation Little Saturn" in order to enlarge the area controlled by the Soviet Army in eastern Ukraine until Kharkov and Rostov.

Zhukov states the South-Western Front was assigned a mission in which the 1st and 3rd Guard armies and the 5th Tank Army "were to strike out in the general direction of Morozovsk and destroy the enemy grouping in that sector." They would be supported by the 6th Army of the Voronezh Front.

First stage: December 1942

The first stage — an attempt to cut off the German Army Group A in the Caucasus — had to be rapidly revised when General Erich von Manstein launched Operation Winter Storm on 12 December in an attempt to relieve the trapped armies at Stalingrad. While General Rodion Malinovsky's Soviet 2nd Guards Army blocked the German advance on Stalingrad, the modified plan *Operation Little Saturn* was launched on 16 December.

This operation consisted of a pincer movement which threatened to cut off the relieving forces. General Fyodor Isidorovich Kuznetsov's 1st Guards Army

Figure 25: *Soviet forces during Operation Little Saturn in December 1942*

and General Dmitri Danilovich Lelyushenko's 3rd Guards Army attacked from the north, encircling 130,000 soldiers of the Italian 8th Army on the Don and advancing to Millerovo. The Italians resisted the Soviet attack for nearly two weeks, although outnumbered 9 to 1 in some sectors, but with huge losses. Manstein sent the 6th Panzer Division to the Italians' aid: of the 130,000 encircled troops, only 45,000 survived after bloody fighting to join the Panzers at Chertkovo on 17 January.

To the south the advance of General Gerasimenko's 28th Army threatened to encircle the 1st Panzer Army and General Trufanov's 51st Army attacked the relief column directly. In a daring raid, by 24 December tanks of the 24th Tank Corps had reached Tatskinskaya, the air base closest to Stalingrad from which the Luftwaffe had been supplying the besieged troops. The Soviet tanks drove through snowstorms onto the airfield and roamed about for hours, destroying the German transport planes at their leisure.

With the relief column under threat of encirclement, Manstein had no choice but to retreat back to Kotelnikovo on 29 December, leaving the encircled Germans at Stalingrad to their fate. Of the 200,000 - 250,000 soldiers encircled 90,000 survived to be taken prisoner. Only 5,000 lived to return to Germany. The limited scope of the Soviet offensive also gave General Ewald von Kleist time to withdraw his Army Group A in the direction of the Kuban, with the exception of 1st Panzer Army which joined Army Group Don via Rostov.

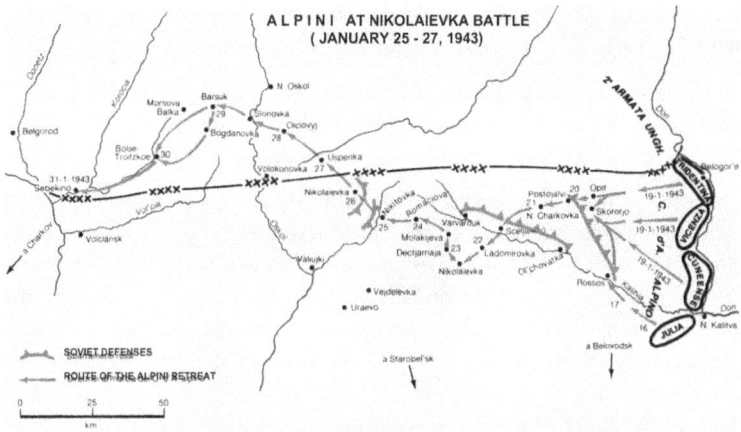

Figure 26: *Route of the Alpini toward Nikolaievka*

Second stage: January 1943

The second stage of operations opened on 13 January 1943 with an attack by four armies of General Golikov's Voronezh Front that encircled and destroyed the Hungarian Second Army near Svoboda on the Don. As a consequence the Hungarian Second Army, as most other Axis armies in the Army Group B, ceased to represent a meaningful fighting force (indeed the German Sixth Army, encircled in Stalingrad, was destroyed on February 2, 1943)

The Italian 8th Army's Alpini Corps, consisting of Alpine Divisions 3rd Julia, 2nd Tridentina and 4th Cuneense and the 156th *Vicenza* Infantry Division to their rear, were at this point largely unaffected by the Soviet offensive on their right flank. But on January 13, 1943, the Soviets launched their second stage of Operation Saturn, where four armies of Soviet General Filipp Golikov's Voronezh Front attacked, encircled, and destroyed the Hungarian Second Army near Svoboda on the Don to the northwest of the Italians. The Soviets then attacked and pushed back the remaining units of the German 24th Army Corps on the Alpini left flank and contemporarily attacked the Alpini themselves.

The Alpini held the front, but within three days the Soviets advanced 200 kilometers (120 mi) to the left and right of the Alpini, who were thus encircled and forced to try to escape a siege (like the one of German sixth Army in Stalingrad).

Although the Alpini corps was ordered to hold the front at all costs, preparations for a general retreat began on January 15. On the evening of January 17, the commanding officer of the corps General Gabriele Nasci finally ordered the full retreat, which was fully carried out on January 19.

At this point the Julia and Cuneense divisions were already heavily decimated and only the Tridentina division was still capable of conducting effective combat operations (Battle of Nikolayevka, January 25–27).

By February first the Alpini reached the Kharkov area, where the Axis forces successfully organized a line of defense. But they did pay a high price in the Soviet Union. The 4 Alpine Division Cuneense was annihilated. Only about one tenth of the 3 Alpine Division Julia survived (approximately 1200 survivors of 15000 troops deployed) and only about one third of the 2 Alpine Division Tridentina survived (approximately 4250 survivors of 15000 troops deployed).

Voronezh-Kastornensk operation

An attack on the German 2nd Army further north threatened to bring about an encirclement; although the German 2nd Army managed to escape, it was forced to retreat and by 5 February troops of the Voronezh Front were approaching Kursk and Kharkov.

Bibliography

<templatestyles src="Template:Refbegin/styles.css" />

* Beevor, Antony (1998). *Stalingrad: The Fateful Siege: 1942–1943*. Harmondsworth, United Kingdom: Penguin Putnam Inc. ISBN 0-670-87095-1.
* Bell, Kelly (Fall 2006). "Struggle for Stalin's Skies". *WWII History: Russian Front*. Herndon, Virginia: Sovereign Media. Special Issue. 1539-5456.
* Clark, Alan (1965). *Barbarossa: The Russian-German Conflict, 1941-1945*. New York City, New York: William Morrow. ISBN 0-688-04268-6.
* Cooper, Matthew (1978). *The German Army 1933-1945*. Lanham, Maryland: Scarborough House. ISBN 0-8128-8519-8.
* Erickson, John (1983). *The Road to Berlin: Stalin's War with Germany*. Yale University Press. ISBN 0-300-07813-7.
* Erickson, John (1975). *The Road to Stalingrad: Stalin's War With Germany*. Yale University Press. ISBN 0-300-07812-9.
* Glantz, David M. (January 1996). "Soviet Military Strategy During the Second Period of War (November 1942–December 1943): A Reappraisal". *The Journal of Military History*. Society for Military History. **60** (1): 35. doi: 10.2307/2944451[231].

- Glantz, David M.; Jonathan House (1995). *When Titans Clashed: How the Red Army Stopped Hitler*. Lawrence, Kansas: Kansas University Press. ISBN 0-7006-0717-X.
- Heiber, Helmut; David M. Glantz (2003). *Hitler and his Generals: Military Conferences 1942 - 1945*. New York City, New York: Enigma Books. ISBN 1-929631-09-X.
- McCarthy, Peter; Mike Syryon (2002). *Panzerkieg: The Rise and Fall of Hitler's Tank Divisions*. New York City, New York: Carroll & Graf. ISBN 0-7867-1009-8.
- McTaggart, Pat (Fall 2006). "Soviet Circle of Iron". *WWII History: Russian Front*. Herndon, Virginia: Sovereign Media. Special Issue. 1539-5456.
- Raus, Erhard (2002). *Panzers on the Eastern Front: General Erhard Raus and his Panzer Divisions in Russia 1941–1945*. Mechanicsburg, PA: Military Book Club. ISBN 0-7394-2644-3.
- von Manstein, Erich (1982). *Lost Victories*. St. Paul, MN: Zenith Press. ISBN 0-7603-2054-3.

Soviet victory

Operation Koltso

Operation *Ring*	
Part of Battle of Stalingrad, Eastern Front, World War II	

Soviet flag over Stalingrad. February 1943

Date	10 January – 2 February 1943
Location	Stalingrad
Result	Soviet victory

Belligerents	
Soviet Union	Germany Romania

Commanders and leaders	
Konstantin Rokossovsky	Friedrich Paulus

Strength	
212,000 troops 6,860 guns and mortars 257 tanks 300 aircraft[232]	250,000 soldiers 4,130 guns and mortars 300 tanks 100 aircraft[232]

Operation Koltso (**Operation Ring**) was the last part of the Battle of Stalingrad. It resulted in the capitulation of the remaining Axis forces encircled in the city.

The attack

The operation was launched on 10 January 1943 with a mass artillery bombardment of the German positions outside the city by the seven encircling
Soviet armies. In the first three days, the Soviets lost 26,000 men and over
half their tanks.[233] The western half of the Stalingrad pocket had been lost by
17 January.

On the 10th, it became clear the main goal was the Pitomnik airfield. "The
44th, 76th and 28th (Motorised) Infantry Divisions were badly hit." The 3rd
(Motorised) Infantry Division, deployed on the southwestern corner of the
cauldron since the end of Nov. 1942, was ordered to retreat to new defensive
positions to avoid encirclement.

The fighting then paused for four days while the Soviet forces regrouped and
redeployed for the next phase of the operation. The second phase of the offensive began on 20 January with a Soviet push toward the airfield at Gumrak.
Two days later, the airfield was occupied by the Soviets. Its capture meant an
end to the evacuation of the German wounded and that any further air supply
would have to be by parachute.

Paulus on 22 January sent a radio message to OKH:

> *Russians in action in 6 km wide on both sides Voroponovo, some with
> flags unfurled to the east. No way to close the gap. Withdrawal to neigh-
> boring fronts who are also without ammunition, useless and not feasi-
> ble. Supply with ammunition from other fronts also no longer possible.
> Food at an end. More than 12,000 unprovided for wounded in the encir-
> clement. What orders shall I give the troops who have no more ammuni-
> tion and will be further attacked with heavy artillery, tanks and massed
> infantry? Fastest decision necessary because dissolution in some places
> already started. Confidence in the leadership still exists.*

The Axis retreated back into the city itself. But resistance to the Soviet advance
gradually diminished due to the exhaustion of all supplies on the Axis side.
On 25 January, LI Corps commander Walther von Seydlitz-Kurzbach told his
divisional commanders to decide for themselves on the matter of surrender.
He was immediately relieved of his command by Paulus. Seydlitz-Kurzbach
later fled the German lines under German fire and personally surrendered to
the Soviets.[234]

On 26 January, detachments of 21st Army met up with the 13th Guards Division to the north of the Mamaev Kurgan, which cut the Axis pocket in Stalingrad in two. Paulus and many of his senior German commanders were in the
smaller southern pocket based in the city center of Stalingrad. The northern

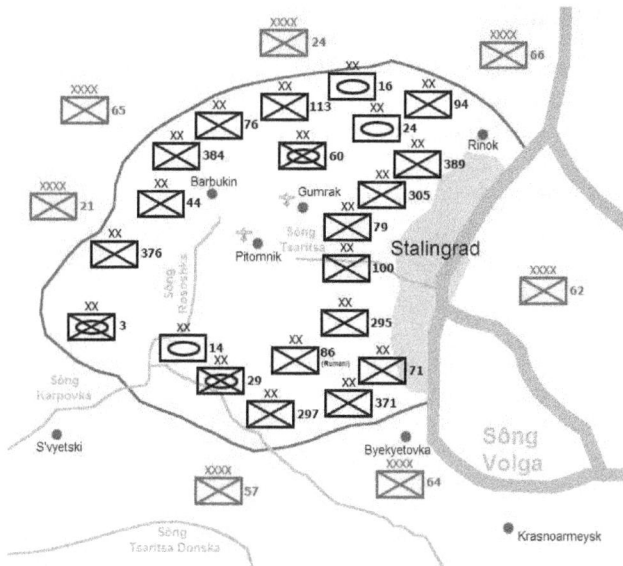

Figure 27: *Disposition of forces in and around Stalingrad.*

pocket was led by XI Corps commander General Strecker and centered in the area around the tractor factory.

In bitter fighting, the Soviets gradually cleared the city center. By 31 January, German resistance in the southern pocket was confined to individual buildings. Soviet forces reached Paulus's headquarters in the Univermag Department Store and the remaining German soldiers ceased their resistance. Soviet Staff officers entered the building and negotiated terms with General Schmidt. Paulus refused to participate directly. In Soviet captivity, Paulus denied having surrendered, claiming to have been taken by surprise. He refused to issue an order to the remaining Germans in the southern pocket to surrender. He also denied having the authority to issue an order for the northern pocket to surrender.[235]

The entire Soviet force at Stalingrad now concentrated on the northern pocket. Intense artillery fire was used to reduce resistance. Soviet forces then followed up, destroying any remaining bunkers, often with direct fire at short range from tanks or artillery. General Strecker continued to resist based on the idea that tying down the Soviet armies at Stalingrad as long as possible would help the German situation elsewhere in the Soviet Union.

The battle ends

By the early morning of 2 February, Strecker was informed that one of his officers had gone to negotiate surrender terms with the Soviets. He then decided to put an end to the fighting. He sent a radio message to Germany, saying that his command had performed its duty to the last man and then surrendered. Organized Axis resistance in the city ended.

Appendix

References

[1] Holt (2009), p. 47.
[2] Liedtke 2016, p. 228.
[3] Antill (2007), pp. 24–25.
[4] Liedtke 2016, p. 230.
[5] Bergström 2007, pp. 49–50.
[6] Mercatante 2012, p. 151.
[7] Schramm (1963), p. 460.
[8] Antill (2007), p. 40.
[9] Antill (2007), pp. 7–12.
[10] Glantz (1995), pp. 108–110.
[11] Wegner (1990), p. 761.
[12] Hayward (2001), p. 2.
[13] Axworthy (1995), p. 19.
[14] Hayward (2001), pp. xvii, 2–5, 18.
[15] Bellamy 2007, p. 497.
[16] Glantz (1995), pp. 111–113.
[17]
[18] Glantz (1995), p. 110.
[19] Hayward (2001), p. 131.
[20]
[21] Wegner (1990), pp. 868–869.
[22] Bellamy (2007), p. 498.
[23]
[24] Glantz (1995), p. 301.
[25] Antill (2007), p. 34.
[26] Antill (2007), p. 37.
[27] Antill (2007), p. 49.
[28] Beevor (1999), p. 75.
[29] Hayward (2001), p. 135.
[30] Bergström 2007, pp. 60, list of Red Air Force order of battle indicates these units were mainly in combat during *Blau*, pp. 49–50.
[31] Glantz (2009), pp. 149–53.
[32] Hayward (2001), p. 142.
[33] Hayward (2001), p. 143.
[34] Hayward (2001), pp. 147, 149.
[35] Glantz (1995), p. 119.
[36] Liddell Hart 1948, pp. 204–205.
[37] Hayward (2001), p. 145.
[38] Bergström 2007, p. 67.
[39] Antill (2007), p. 41.
[40] Hayward (2001), p. 156.
[41] Hayward (2001), p. 152.
[42] Glantz (1995), p. 121.
[43] Antill (2007), p. 39.
[44] Liddell Hart 1948, pp. 201–203.
[45] Hayward (2001), p. 147.
[46] Liddell Hart 1948, p. 202.
[47] Glantz (1995), p. 120.
[48] Glantz (1995), p. 122.
[49] Antill (2007), pp. 13–14.

[50] Schramm (1963), p. 583.
[51] Schramm (1963), p. 639.
[52] Hayward (2001), p. 167.
[53] Wegner (1990), p. 942-953.
[54] Hayward (2001), p. 169.
[55] Hayward (2001), p. 170.
[56] Schramm (1963), p. 667.
[57] Schramm (1963), pp. 639, 671.
[58] Hayward (2001), p. 171.
[59] Spencer C. Tucker, *World War II: The Definitive Encyclopedia and Document Collection (5 volumes)*, ABC-CLIO, 2016, p. 1422 https//books.google.ro
[60] Schramm (1963), p. 65. and Hayward (2001), p. 174.
[61] Schramm (1963), pp. 719–723.
[62] Hayward (2001), p. 172.
[63] Hayward (2001), p. 179.
[64] Bergström 2007, p. 84.
[65] Hayward (2001), pp. 179–180.
[66] Hayward 1995, pp. 94–135.
[67] Antill (2007), pp. 44–45.
[68] Bergström 2007, p. 62.
[69] Antill p. 49.
[70] Beevor (1999), p. 106.
[71] Bergström 2007, p. 73.
[72] Antill (2007), pp. 45–51.
[73] Beevor (1999), pp. 115–118.
[74] Antill (2007), p. 55.
[75] Antill (2007), pp. 51–67.
[76] Glantz (1995), pp. 122–123, 149.
[77] Axworthy (1995), pp. 85–89.
[78] Antill (2007), pp. 73–75.
[79] Glantz (1995), p. 134.
[80] Nipe (2000), p. 15.
[81] Glantz (1995), pp. 140–141.
[82] Antill (2007), p. 78.
[83] Nipe (2000), pp. 18–21.
[84] Schramm (1963), p. 1318.
[85]
[86]
[87]
[88] Vego, Milan N. *Naval Strategy and Operations in Narrow Seas* (MPG Books Ltd, London, 2003), p. 278.
[89] Glantz (1995), p. 141.
[90] Glantz (1995), p. 132.
[91] Antill (2007), p. 43.
[92]
[93] http://czechout.org/journal/135.pdf
[94] //www.worldcat.org/issn/0142-3525
[95] Infanterie Regiment 369 (kroatisches) http://www.axishistory.com/index.php?id=2158 Axis history forum, accessed: 19 March 2009
[96] http://www.lexikon-der-wehrmacht.de/
[97] http://www.stalingradbattle.nl/personen/personen.htm
[98] http://www.axishistory.com/index.php?id=2076
[99] https://web.archive.org/web/20090320221210/http://lexikon-der-wehrmacht.de/Karte/Stalingrad3.htm
[100] http://www.staldata.com/index.php
[101] Beevor (1998)

[102] Командующие воздушными армиями ВВС РККА в период 1942—1945 гг. http://www.
soldat.ru/force/sssr/rkka/vvs/06_komva.html
[103] Hayward 1998, p. 151.
[104] Hayward 1998, p. 183.
[105] Hayward 1998, pp. 185–186.
[106] Hayward 1998, p. 187.
[107] Hayward 1998, p. 188.
[108] Bergstrom, Christer ; "Stalingrad: The Air Battle 1942 Through January 1943" : page 72.
[109] Hayward 1998, pp. 188–189.
[110] Hayward 1998, p. 189.
[111] Bergström 2007b, p. 73.
[112] Hayward 1998, pp. 190–191.
[113] Hayward 1998, pp. 194–196.
[114] //tools.wmflabs.org/geohack/geohack.php?pagename=Operation_Uranus&params=48_42_N_
44_31_E_type:event
[115] //doi.org/10.2307/2944451
[116] http://www.staldata.com/oob.php
[117] "Germany at War: 400 Years of Military History", p. 1467.
[118] "Germany at War: 400 Years of Military History", p. 1467.
[119] "Germany at War: 400 Years of Military History", p. 1467.
[120] McCarthy & Syron (2002), p. 141
[121] Erickson (1983), p. 4
[122] Glantz (1995), p. 134
[123] Glantz (1995), pp. 134–136
[124] Erickson (1983), p. 7
[125] Erickson (1983), p. 3
[126] Bell (2006), p. 62
[127] Bell (2006), pp. 62–63
[128] Bell (2006), p. 63
[129] Erickson (1975), p. 472
[130] Glantz (1996), p. 118
[131] Erickson (1975), p. 470
[132] Erickson (1975), pp. 470–471
[133] McCarthy & Syron (2002), p. 143
[134] Erickson (1983), p. 8
[135] Erickson (1975), p. 471
[136] Beevor (1998), pp. 292–293
[137] Erickson (1983), p. 9
[138] McCarthy & Syron (2002), pp. 143–144
[139] Erickson (1983), pp. 7–8
[140] von Manstein (1982), p. 318
[141] von Mansten (1982), pp. 319–320
[142] von Manstein (1982), p. 320
[143] Erickson (1983), p. 10
[144] Erickson (1983), pp. 10–11
[145] McCarthy & Syron (2002), p. 144
[146] Erickson (1983), p. 11
[147] von Manstein (1982), pp. 318–319
[148] von Manstein (1982), p. 319
[149] Clark (1965), pp. 258–259
[150] Cooper (1978), p. 428
[151] Cooper (1978), pp. 428–429
[152] Clark (1965), p. 259
[153] Cooper (1978), p. 429
[154] Clark (1965), pp. 259–260
[155] Clark (1965), pp. 260–261

[156] Clark (1965), p. 261
[157] Clark (1965), pp. 261–263
[158] Clark (1965), p. 264
[159] Clark (1965), pp. 264–265
[160] Clark (1965), p. 265
[161] Clark (1965), p. 266
[162] McTaggart (2006), p. 50
[163] Erickson (1975), p. 457
[164] Erickson (1975), p. 462
[165] Glantz (1996), p. 121
[166] McCarthy & Syron (2002), p. 145
[167] McCarthy & Syron (2002), pp. 145–146
[168] Beevor (1998), p. 298
[169] Raus (2002), p. 128
[170] Isaev (2008), p. 365
[171] Raus (2002), pp. 128–129
[172] von Manstein (1982), pp. 330–331
[173] Heiber & Glantz (2003), p. 22
[174] Raus (2002), p. 147
[175] This included a number of flame-thrower KV-8 tanks which were intended to be used in the street fighting in Stalingrad, and were not on par with the German Panzer IV tanks; Isaev (2008), p. 372
[176] Raus (2002), pp. 147–149
[177] Raus (2002), p. 149
[178] Joly (2017), p. 171
[179] Joly (2017), p. 173
[180] Raus (2002), pp. 147–156
[181] Raus (2002), p. 156–158
[182] Raus (2002), p. 158
[183] Beevor (1998), pp. 298–299
[184] Raus (2002), pp. 158–159
[185] Erickson (1983), pp. 12–13
[186] Isaev (2008), pp. 369–370
[187] Erickson (1983), p. 13
[188] Beevor (1998), p. 299
[189] Erickson (1983), pp. 13–14
[190] Erickson (1983), pp. 14–15
[191] Beevor (1998), pp. 299–300
[192] Beevor (1998), p. 300
[193] Beevor (1998), p. 301
[194] Erickson (1983), p. 18
[195] Beevor (1998), pp. 301–302
[196] von Manstein (1982), p. 331
[197] Erickson (1983), p. 15
[198] von Manstein (1982), pp. 331–332
[199] Glantz (1995), p. 140
[200] von Manstein (1982), p. 332
[201] von Manstein (1982), pp. 332–333
[202] von Manstein (1982), pp. 333–334
[203] von Manstein (1982), p. 334
[204] von Manstein (1982), pp. 334–335
[205] von Manstein (1982), pp. 335–336
[206] Beevor (1998), pp. 309–310
[207] Erickson (1982), p. 22
[208] McCarthy & Syron (2002), p. 148
[209] Erickson (1983), pp. 22–23

[210]Glantz (1995), pp. 140–141
[211]
[212]Erickson (1983), pp. 23–24
[213]McCarthy & Syron (2002), p. 149
[214]McCarthy & Syron (2002), pp. 149–150
[215]Erickson (1983), p. 25
[216]Glantz (1995), p. 141
[217]Erickson (1983), p. 27
[218]Cooper (1978), p. 436
[219]Erickson (1983), pp. 28–29
[220]Glantz (1995), pp. 141–152
[221]//doi.org/10.2307/2944451
[222]//www.jstor.org/stable/2944451
[223]Glantz (1997), p. 116
[224]Glantz (1997), p. 117
[225]Cooper (1978), pp. 415–416
[226]McCarthy & Syron (2002), p. 132
[227]Erickson (1975), p. 362
[228]Beevor (1998), p. 84
[229]Glantz (1997), pp. 119–120
[230]Glantz (1997), p. 120
[231]//doi.org/10.2307/2944451
[232]*The Great Patriotic War of the Soviet Union, 1941-1945. A Brief History*, pp. 198-199
[233]*Stalingrad* (Beevor), p. 356
[234]*Stalingrad* (Beevor), p. 382
[235]*Stalingrad* (Beevor), p. 390

Article Sources and Contributors

The sources listed for each article provide more detailed licensing information including the copyright status, the copyright owner, and the license conditions.

Case Blue *Source:* https://en.wikipedia.org/w/index.php?oldid=853741931 *License:* Creative Commons Attribution-Share Alike 3.0 *Contributors:* Adavidb, Adel.M.Radwan, Adûnâi, Aleksandr Grigoryev, Anotherclown, Arjayay, AustralianRupert, Bender235, Boscaswell, Brufnus, Buckshot06, Central Data Bank, Chrisknop, Clarityfiend, ClueBot NG, CommonsDelinker, Concertmusic, D2306, Danrok, Dapi89, Davidcannon, Dead Mary, Denniss, Ehistory, Ezhiki, Ferroequus, Gaius Cornelius, GeneralizationsAreBad, Gog the Mild, GoodDay, Grant65, Gunbirddriver, Hairy Dude, Hamish59, Hmains, Irondome, Italia2006, J S Phillip, JamesRussels, Jan Hoellwarth, Jdaloner, Jop2∼enwiki, K.e.coffman, Keith-264, Khazar, Kintetsubuffalo, Laero, Lieutcoluseng, Mabandalone, Maranello Prime, Math321, MiG29VN, MisterBee1966, Mojoworker, Nazgul02, Newzild, Niceguyedc, Nicolas Perrault III, Oceanyes, Ori Livneh, PBS, Peacemaker67, Philg88, PhnomPencil, Pi3.124, Piledhigheranddeeper, Redrose64, Romanian-and-proud, Rrostrom, Russ3Z, Ryanbrz, Sca, Sergii.Fiot, Slawekb, Snapperman2, Snorvege, Spicemix, Spyglasses, Sturwarsbv, Sturmvogel 66, The PIPE, The Rambling Man, Thommy9, TiltuM, Tom.Reding, Torpilorul, Trekphiler, Truthanado, TwinkleMore, Utahwriter14, Valenciano, Vgy7ujm, VivaSlava, Vmavanti, White Shadows, WilliamJE, Winterst, Yunccha92, ÅDA - DÅP, Ψ, 112 anonymous edits

Axis order of battle at the Battle of Stalingrad *Source:* https://en.wikipedia.org/w/index.php?oldid=819197393 *License:* Creative Commons Attribution-Share Alike 3.0 *Contributors:* D2306, Ereinon, Farawayman, Jmg38, Kges1901, Marcocapelle, Nazgul02, Nickst, Nyttend, Ryan.opel, Topbanana, Trident13, Wreck Smurfy, Zloyvolsheb, 8 anonymous edits 23

Soviet order of battle for the Battle of Stalingrad *Source:* https://en.wikipedia.org/w/index.php?oldid=817992628 *License:* Creative Commons Attribution-Share Alike 3.0 *Contributors:* Aleksander Kaasik, Bahavd Gita, Bgwhite, Bob1960evens, Buckshot06, CWenger, ChrisGualtieri, Davidcannon, D12000, Ereinon, Farawayman, Jmg38, Kges1901, Marcocapelle, Nazgul02, Nickst, Nyttend, Ryan.opel, Topbanana, Trident13, Wreck Smurfy, Zloyvolsheb, 8 anonymous edits 26

Bombing of Stalingrad *Source:* https://en.wikipedia.org/w/index.php?oldid=841301025 *License:* Creative Commons Attribution-Share Alike 3.0 *Contributors:* BD2412, ClueBot NG, Colonies Chris, DagosNavy, Dapi89, DocGratis, Epolk, Fleebo, GeorgeofOrange, GrahamBould, Grutness, Harryurz, Hyperbolick, Joe N, John of Reading, K.e.coffman, LWG, MBK004, Mrg3105, Nekohakase, O keyes, Oshwah, Salish88, The Anomebot2, TiltuM, Tswold@msn.com, Ultraviolet scissor flame, Wrp103, 20 anonymous edits 31

Operation Uranus *Source:* https://en.wikipedia.org/w/index.php?oldid=853943905 *License:* Creative Commons Attribution-Share Alike 3.0 *Contributors:* 4wajzkd02, 564dude, A little insignificant, Acroterion, AdmiralKolchak, Ain92, Alansohn, Alasto Light, Andrew Gray, Anotherclown, Art LaPella, Arturspipars, AstaBOTh15, AustralianRupert, BOTarate, Betamw, Bleakcomb, Blueyays, BokicaK, Bongwarrior, Brandmeister (old), Brufnus, Buckshot06, CaptainFugu, CardinalDan, Catalan, Chiswick Chap, Christwelfwww, Citation bot 1, ClueBot NG, ColorOfSuffering, CommonsDelinker, DadaNeem, Dana boomer, Dapi89, David R. Ingham, DavidCane, DavisGL, Dawn Bard, Dead Mary, Denniss, Dodo19∼enwiki, Don Argus jr, Dr. Klim, DrKay, East718, Egmontaz, Eik Corell, Emw, Er Cicero, Ericoides, Esdrasbarnevelt, EyeSerene, Farnspear, Fateslieutenant, Fieldday-sunday, Giants2008, Googlehoops, Gottenbr, GrahamBould, Gravies123456789, HaeB, Hamish59, HieraticalWatchman, Hohum, Howcheng, Hux, ladmc, Interchange88, Ironholds, Italia2006, Ixfd64, J.delanoy, Jappalang, Javert, Jdaloner, Jmg38, Joe iNsecure, Josullivan.59, Juliancolton, K.e.coffman, KariM, Kges1901, Kingpin13, Kirill Lokshin, Kiwifist, Lacrimosus, Laero, LeinSora, Llamalover242, LoanP8, Lorackio, LovesMacs, Lt.Pearson, LtNOWIS, MJ1996, Mareklug, Maxaxax, Mhman, Michael Devore, Mild Bill Hiccup, MisterBee1966, Mm40, NawlinWiki, Niceguyedc, Nick-D, Nicolas Perrault III, Old Moonraker, Omnipaedista, Paul Erik, PaulinSaudi, Pi3.124, Piledhigheranddeeper, Pirastedan, Pol098, Pusegona, Rcbutcher, Recognizance, Rich Farmbrough, Richard David Ramsey, Rjwilmsi, Robertiki, RockMFR, Romanian-and-proud, Ronnotel, Ryan.opel, SS451, SandyGeorgia, Skunkboy74, Sonofswirk, Spinner145, Squid661, Sun Creator, Tabletop, The Anomebot2, The Thing That Should Not Be, The ed17, Theleftorium, Tim!, Tom.Reding, Trekphiler, Truthanado, Twas Now, TwinkleMore, Udafed, Uncle Dick, Ur my cousin azooz im sorry, Vicenarian, Vietbook, Vincinio, Volker89, Vpab15, WBritten, WereSpielChequers, WilliamJE, WolfmanSF, WorldWarTwoEditor, Yarnalgo, Yelizandpaul, ZCman1217, 153 anonymous edits 1

Operation Winter Storm *Source:* https://en.wikipedia.org/w/index.php?oldid=848265748 *License:* Creative Commons Attribution-Share Alike 3.0 *Contributors:* 23 editor, AadaamS, Aeonx, Alyssa hoffel, Andreas1968, Andres, Asav, Bernd.Brincken, Betamw, Bobby D. Bryant, Bryan Derksen, Buckshot06, Capt Jim, CaptainFugu, Catalan, Charlesdrakew, Chilrreh, Chris the speller, Citation bot 1, Clarityfiend, Concertmusic, DJ Clayworth, DMorpheus, DO'Neil, Dead Mary, DI2000, Dodo19∼enwiki, El C, Ericoides, Gdr, Gits (Neo), GregorB, Hamish59, HopsonRoad, Irondome, JackofOz, James-Russels, Jason Recliner, Esq., Jdaloner, JustinSmith, Jwy, K.e.coffman, Keith-264, Khazar2, Kjetvolk, Koavf, Lexlythius, LoanP8, MBK004, Magus732, MastCell, Mhardcastle, Michael Devore, Michael Dorosh, MisterBee1966, Mrg3105, Newzild, Niceguyedc, Oberiko, Owain Knight, Paul Siebert, PhnomPencil, Physicistjedi, Pi3.124, Pikazilla, Pibotgourou, R5452, Rafairminded, RedWolf, Regione, Rjwilmsi, Rmhermen, Robert1947, Roger Davies, Romanian-and-proud, SandyGeorgia, Sardaka, Scholar-correction-wiki, Spot87, The Anomebot2, The Banner Turbo, The Evil Spartan, The Rambling Man, The ed17, Tim!, TimVickers, Tirronan, Tom.Reding, Tybradbury, Tswold@msn.com, TwinkleMore, Ucucha, Vermondo, Volker89, Wandalstouring, WereSpielChequers, WhaleyTim, Witchchester, WorldWarTwoEditor, Wwoods, ÅDA - DÅP, 66 anonymous edits 55

Operation Little Saturn *Source:* https://en.wikipedia.org/w/index.php?oldid=845420634 *License:* Creative Commons Attribution-Share Alike 3.0 *Contributors:* Adel.M.Radwan, AlexR, Alexander Tendler, Alfiuman, Altenmann, Andreas1968, Attilios, BBuchbinder, BlckKnght, Broux, Bryan Derksen, Catalan, Central Data Bank, Cmskog, Colonel Cow, CommonsDelinker, D2306, Danvintius Bookix∼enwiki, Dchris1990, De Riban5, Dead Mary, Dodo19∼enwiki, DonaldGump, Driftwoodzebulin, Ericoides, Ferruccio Vio, Filiep, Fireaxe888, Fuhghettaboutit, Gdr, George Burgess, GoodDay, Ground Zero, Hamish59, JackofOz, Jayanta Sen, Jdaloner, K.e.coffman, KD53, KNewman, Kevinsam, Laidita, LoanP8, Lucifero4, Luckyz, MBK004, MisterBee1966, Mkpumphrey, Mrg3105, Oberiko, PasswordUsername, PaulinSaudi, Peterdx, Phoenix-wiki, Pi3.124, Pluke, R'n'B, Realmmb, Rjwilmsi, Robertiki, Romanian-and-proud, SEM, Sigurd von Kleist, Taeguk, The Anome, The Anomebot2, Thommy9, Tim!, Tom.Reding, Tswold@msn.com, TuxLibNit, TwinkleMore, Ulflarsen, Vina-iwbot∼enwiki, Wendell, White Shadows, WilliamJE, WorldWarTwoEditor, Wwoods, Yanksox, ZappaOMati, 56 anonymous edits 67

Operation Koltso *Source:* https://en.wikipedia.org/w/index.php?oldid=833157904 *License:* Creative Commons Attribution-Share Alike 3.0 *Contributors:* Altenmann, Angusmclellan, Bearcat, Bethpage89, Christwelfwww, Clarityfiend, D2306, I dream of horses, Jdaloner, Keith-264, Nick-D, Nneonneo, Oaklandguy, PhnomPencil, Pi3.124, Spuggly, Taeguk, The Anomebot2, Tom.Reding, TwinkleMore, Whoop whoop pull up, 14 anonymous edits 75

Image Sources, Licenses and Contributors

The sources listed for each image provide more detailed licensing information including the copyright status, the copyright owner, and the license conditions.

Image *Source:* https://en.wikipedia.org/w/index.php?title=File:Bundesarchiv_Bild_101I-218-0503-19,_Russland-Süd,_zerstörter_russischer_Panzer.jpg *License:* Creative Commons Attribution-Sharealike 3.0 Germany *Contributors:* BotMultichill, Bukvoed, Denniss, Gunbirddriver2, Martin H., SuperTank17, Wieralee ... 1

Image *Source:* https://en.wikipedia.org/w/index.php?title=File:Flag_of_German_Reich_(1935–1945).svg *Contributors:* - ... 1

Image *Source:* https://en.wikipedia.org/w/index.php?title=File:Flag_of_Italy_(1861-1946)_crowned.svg *License:* Creative Commons Attribution-Sharealike 2.5 *Contributors:* F l a n k e r ... 1

Image *Source:* https://en.wikipedia.org/w/index.php?title=File:Flag_of_Romania.svg *Contributors:* AdiJapan ... 1

Image *Source:* https://en.wikipedia.org/w/index.php?title=File:Flag_of_Hungary_(1915-1918,_1919-1946).svg *License:* Creative Commons Zero *Contributors:* User:Zscout370, colour correction: User:R-41, current version: Thommy ... 1

Image *Source:* https://en.wikipedia.org/w/index.php?title=File:Flag_of_Independent_State_of_Croatia.svg *License:* Public domain *Contributors:* public domain by User:Zscout370 ... 1

Image *Source:* https://en.wikipedia.org/w/index.php?title=File:Flag_of_First_Slovak_Republic_1939-1945.svg *Contributors:* - ... 1

Image *Source:* https://en.wikipedia.org/w/index.php?title=File:Flag_of_the_Soviet_Union_(1936–1955).svg *License:* GNU Free Documentation License *Contributors:* User:Rotemliss ... 1

Image *Source:* https://en.wikipedia.org/w/index.php?title=File:War_Ensign_of_Germany_1938-1945.svg *Contributors:* - ... 1

Figure 1 *Source:* https://en.wikipedia.org/w/index.php?title=File:Bundesarchiv_Bild_101III-Altstadt-055-12,_Russland,_SS-Division_Wiking_beim_Vormarsch.jpg *License:* Creative Commons Attribution-Sharealike 3.0 Germany *Contributors:* BotMultichill, Bragidier, Denniss, Fastboy, Gandvik ... 5

Figure 2 *Source:* https://en.wikipedia.org/w/index.php?title=File:Eastern_Front_1942-05_to_1942-11.png *License:* GNU Free Documentation License *Contributors:* User:Gdr ... 7

Figure 3 *Source:* https://en.wikipedia.org/w/index.php?title=File:Bundesarchiv_Bild_101I-217-0494-34,_Russland-Süd,_Schützenpanzer.jpg *License:* Creative Commons Attribution-Sharealike 3.0 Germany *Contributors:* BotMultichill, Cobatfor, GT1976, Martin H., Morio, SuperTank17 ... 10

Figure 4 *Source:* https://en.wikipedia.org/w/index.php?title=File:Bundesarchiv_Bild_101I-031-2417-09,_Russland,_Kaukasus,_Gebirgsjäger.jpg *License:* Creative Commons Attribution-Sharealike 3.0 Germany *Contributors:* Alonso de Mendoza, BotMultichill, Gkml, Manxruler, Martin H., Pelex, Prüm ... 12

Figure 5 *Source:* https://en.wikipedia.org/w/index.php?title=File:Bundesarchiv_Bild_146-1970-033-04,_Russland,_Kaukasus,_Gebirgsjäger.jpg *License:* Creative Commons Attribution-Sharealike 3.0 Germany *Contributors:* Ain92, Alonso de Mendoza, Bukvoed, Estormiz, Fastboy, Manxruler, Martin H., Prüm ... 13

Figure 6 *Source:* https://en.wikipedia.org/w/index.php?title=File:Bundesarchiv_Bild_101I-218-0510-22,_Russland-Süd,_Panzersoldat.jpg *License:* Creative Commons Attribution-Sharealike 3.0 Germany *Contributors:* Ain92, Avron, BotMultichill, Cirt, Cobatfor, Fallschirmjäger, Gandvik, Jakednb, Laurifindil, Martin H., SuperTank17, Sven Manguard, Vasyatka1, Wieralee, BoенTex, 1 anonymous edits ... 15

Figure 7 *Source:* https://en.wikipedia.org/w/index.php?title=File:Bundesarchiv_Bild_183-J20510,_Russland,_Kampf_um_Stalingrad,_Luftangriff_crop.jpg *License:* Creative Commons Attribution-Sharealike 3.0 Germany *Contributors:* Before My Ken, Jochen Burghardt ... 16

Figure 8 *Source:* https://en.wikipedia.org/w/index.php?title=File:Bundesarchiv_Bild_101I-617-2571-04,_Stalingrad,_Soldaten_beim_Häuserkampf.jpg *License:* Creative Commons Attribution-Sharealike 3.0 Germany *Contributors:* Alonso de Mendoza, Avron, BotMultichill, High Contrast, Martin H., 1 anonymous edits ... 17

Figure 9 *Source:* https://en.wikipedia.org/w/index.php?title=File:Operazione_Piccolo_Saturno.jpg *License:* Public Domain *Contributors:* fotoreporter sovietico sconosciuto ... 19

Figure 10 *Source:* https://en.wikipedia.org/w/index.php?title=File:Stalingrad_Encirclement_it.png *License:* Public Domain *Contributors:* Stalingrad_Encirclement.jpg: Original uploader was ShadeOfGrey at bg.wikipedia derivative work: Luigi Chiesa (talk) ... 24

Figure 11 *Source:* https://en.wikipedia.org/w/index.php?title=File:Stalingrad_Encirclement_it.png *License:* Public Domain *Contributors:* Stalingrad_Encirclement.jpg: Original uploader was ShadeOfGrey at bg.wikipedia derivative work: Luigi Chiesa (talk) ... 27

Figure 12 *Source:* https://en.wikipedia.org/w/index.php?title=File:Bundesarchiv_Bild_183-J17815,_Russland,_Kampf_um_Stalingrad,_Luftangriff.jpg *License:* Creative Commons Attribution-Sharealike 3.0 Germany *Contributors:* BotMultichill, Felix Stember, Leha-11, Martin H., Rcbutcher ... 32

Figure 13 *Source:* https://en.wikipedia.org/w/index.php?title=File:Bundesarchiv_Bild_183-F0703-0217-001,_Russland,_Kesselschlacht_Stalingrad.jpg *License:* Creative Commons Attribution-Sharealike 3.0 Germany *Contributors:* BotMultichill, Felix Stember, Petri Krohn ... 34

Figure 14 *Source:* https://en.wikipedia.org/w/index.php?title=File:Children's_Dance_fountain_in_Stalingrad,_23_August_1942.jpeg *License:* Creative Commons Attribution 3.0 Unported *Contributors:* Andrew M. Vachin, Lotse, Nabak, Tosha, 1 anonymous edits ... 35

Figure 15 *Source:* https://en.wikipedia.org/w/index.php?title=File:Bundesarchiv_Bild_146-1978-093-03,_Stalingrad,_zertörte_Industrieanlage.jpg *License:* Creative Commons Attribution-Sharealike 3.0 Germany *Contributors:* BotMultichill, Felix Stember, Leha-11, Rcbutcher, Wst ... 36

Image *Source:* https://en.wikipedia.org/w/index.php?title=File:Operation_Uranus.svg *License:* Creative Commons Attribution 3.0 *Contributors:* Lưu Ly ... 39

Image *Source:* https://en.wikipedia.org/w/index.php?title=File:Flag_of_Italy_(1861–1946).svg *License:* Creative Commons Attribution-Sharealike 2.5 *Contributors:* F l a n k e r ... 39

Image *Source:* https://en.wikipedia.org/w/index.php?title=File:Flag_of_Hungary_1940.svg *Contributors:* - ... 39

Figure 16 *Source:* https://en.wikipedia.org/w/index.php?title=File:Bundesarchiv_Bild_101I-216-0445-18,_Russland-Mitte-Nord,_Panzer_IV..jpg *License:* Creative Commons Attribution-Sharealike 3.0 Germany *Contributors:* -hax0r, Ain92, BotMultichill, Felix Stember, Hohum, Martin H., Morio, SuperTank17 ... 42

Figure 17 *Source:* https://en.wikipedia.org/w/index.php?title=File:Bundesarchiv_Bild_183-B24575,_Friedrich_Paulus.jpg *License:* Creative Commons Attribution-Sharealike 3.0 Germany *Contributors:* BotMultichill, Bundesarchiv-B6, Fredy.00, M-J, Manxruler, Marcus Cyron, Martin H., Uaauaa, Vizu ... 43

Figure 18 *Source:* https://en.wikipedia.org/w/index.php?title=File:Bundesarchiv_Bild_101I-218-0501-11,_Russland-Süd,_rumänischer_Soldat.jpg *License:* Creative Commons Attribution-Sharealike 3.0 Germany *Contributors:* Ain92, CaptainFugu, Illegitimate Barrister, Laurifindil, Martin H., Mtsmallwood, Olahus, Prüm ... 46

Figure 19 *Source:* https://en.wikipedia.org/w/index.php?title=File:Stalingrad_-_Preparations_for_Operation_Uranus.png *License:* Creative Commons Attribution-Sharealike 3.0 *Contributors:* User:Josullivan.59 ... 47

Figure 20 *Source:* https://en.wikipedia.org/w/index.php?title=File:Bundesarchiv_Bild_101III-Bueschel-090-39,_Russland,_Grenadiere_der_Waffen-SS_beim_Vorgehen.jpg *License:* Creative Commons Attribution-Sharealike 3.0 Germany *Contributors:* BotMultichill, Chiswick Chap, Denniss, Gandvik, Hohum, 1 anonymous edits ... 49

Image *Source:* https://en.wikipedia.org/w/index.php?title=File:Map_Battle_of_Stalingrad-en.svg *License:* Public Domain *Contributors:* iMeowbot 50

Image *Source:* https://en.wikipedia.org/w/index.php?title=File:Commons-logo.svg *License:* logo *Contributors:* Anomie, Callanecc, CambridgeBayWeather, Jo-Jo Eumerus, RHaworth ... 54

Image *Source:* https://en.wikipedia.org/w/index.php?title=File:Cscr-featured.svg *License:* GNU Lesser General Public License *Contributors:* Anomie ... 54

Image *Source:* https://en.wikipedia.org/w/index.php?title=File:Bundesarchiv_Bild_101I-457-0065-36,_Russland,_Panzer_VI_(Tiger_I)_und_T34.jpg *License:* Creative Commons Attribution-Sharealike 3.0 Germany *Contributors:* Ain92, Avron, BotMultichill, Catsmeat, Cirt, Laurifindil, Manxruler, Martin H., Pibwl, SuperTank17, Sven Manguard, Wieralee ... 55

Figure 21 *Source:* https://en.wikipedia.org/w/index.php?title=File:Eastern_Front_1942-11_to_1943-03.png *License:* GNU Free Documentation License *Contributors:* Ain92, Catalan, D2306, Joonasl, Juiced lemon, Lx 121, MGA73bot2, Mahahahaneapneap, OgreBot 2, Sdrtirs, Spiridon Ion Cepleanu, TCY, TFCforever, 1 anonymous edits ... 57

Figure 22 *Source:* https://en.wikipedia.org/w/index.php?title=File:Bundesarchiv_Bild_183-H01757,_Erich_von_Manstein.jpg *License:* Creative Commons Attribution-Sharealike 3.0 Germany *Contributors:* A1B2C3D4, BotMultichill, DIREKTOR, Hohum, Lupo, Mbdortmund, Uaauaa ... 59

Figure 23 *Source:* https://en.wikipedia.org/w/index.php?title=File:Bundesarchiv_Bild_101I-457-0056-12,_Russland-Mitte,_Panzer_VI_(Tiger_I)_in_Ortschaft.jpg *License:* Creative Commons Attribution-Sharealike 3.0 Germany *Contributors:* Ain92, An Errant Knight, Avron, BotMultichill, Brakeet, Catsmeat, High Contrast, Hohum, Ingolfson, Martin H., Wieralee ... 61

Figure 24   *Source:* https://en.wikipedia.org/w/index.php?title=File:Bundesarchiv_Bild_101III-Bueschel-090-39,_Russland,_Grenadiere_der_ Waffen-SS_beim_Vorgehen.jpg   *License:* Creative Commons Attribution-Sharealike 3.0 Germany *Contributors:*   BotMultichill, Chiswick Chap, Denniss, Gandvik, Hohum, 1 anonymous edits 63
Image   *Source:* https://en.wikipedia.org/w/index.php?title=File:Symbol_support_vote.svg   *License:* Public Domain *Contributors:*   Anomie, Fastily, Jo-Jo Eumerus 67
Figure 25 *Source:* https://en.wikipedia.org/w/index.php?title=File:Operazione_Piccolo_Saturno.jpg *License:* Public Domain *Contributors:*   fotore- porter sovietico sconosciuto 70
Figure 26   *Source:* https://en.wikipedia.org/w/index.php?title=File:Ripiegamentoalpinigennaio43.jpg   *License:* Creative Commons Attribution- Sharealike 3.0 *Contributors:*   User:LoanP8 71
Image   *Source:* https://en.wikipedia.org/w/index.php?title=File:Bundesarchiv_Bild_183-W0506-316,_Russland,_Kampf_um_Stalingrad, _Siegesflagge.jpg *License:* Creative Commons Attribution-Sharealike 3.0 Germany *Contributors:*   Ain92, Aleksej fon Grozni, BotMultichill, Catsmeat, Fastboy, Guandalug, Hohum, Look2See1, Манхруler, Markscheider, Moehre1992, Mogelzahn, Raymond, Василий Геннадиевич, 1 anonymous edits 75
Figure 27 *Source:* https://en.wikipedia.org/w/index.php?title=File:Stalingrad_Encirclement(vi).jpg *License:* Public Domain *Contributors:*   Original uploader was at bg.wikipedia 77

License

Index